The Financial Fitness Blueprint

A Practical Guide for Creating the Life You Want by Taking Charge of Your Money

Courtney Carroll
—The Financial Fitness Trainer

iUniverse, Inc.
Bloomington

The Financial Fitness Blueprint
A Practical Guide for Creating the Life You
Want by Taking Charge of Your Money

iUniverse books may be ordered through booksellers or by contacting:

iUniverse
1663 Liberty Drive
Bloomington, IN 47403
www.iuniverse.com
1-800-Authors (1-800-288-4677)

ISBN: 978-1-4759-4225-5 (sc)
ISBN: 978-1-4759-4227-9 (hc)
ISBN: 978-1-4759-4226-2 (e)

Printed in the United States of America
iUniverse rev. date: 07/20/2012

Acknowledgements

A few people deserve special recognition for their role in shaping my philosophy and helping me move my life in the direction of my chief aim.

I would first like to thank my mom for her unwavering belief in me. Thank you for your prayers and encouragement throughout the writing of this book. You have been my strongest supporter, always in my corner cheering me on with 100 percent conviction and confidence. To you I dedicate this book. I thank you for your love and blessings over the years and know this book would not be possible without the valuable lessons you've taught. I love you dearly.

To my mentor and coach Paola Breda of Canadian Financial Freedom, you have been an inspiration and a true blessing to me. You helped me see beyond my limiting beliefs and encouraged me to take charge of my life. Your commitment to others and selflessness have been etched in my mind and inspired me to follow in your footsteps and be a beacon of hope to others. Your expertise in finance and real estate investing has helped change countless lives and you continue to give passionately to others so they can achieve financial freedom. Your heart is big and your passion for helping others is unmatched. May you continue to be blessed and your rewards grow exponentially.

To my sister Audrey, thank you for your support and prayers over the years. You put your trust in me to walk the road less travelled in order to change our lives and that of our family. Most importantly, you put your money where your mouth is and believed in me before I was a proven real estate investor. You are an inspiration to me and I am grateful for the guidance and wisdom you have provided.

To Shirley Ho, you too have been an inspiration and a great friend through the years. I love your energy and enthusiasm to go after the things you want in life. At age 26 you have already put yourself in a position to finish way ahead of the crowd. Your commitment to creating a financially fit future so you can bless others should serve as an example for others your age. I wish you continued success.

Writing a book appears to be an individual project, but if you want it to be read by thousands or hopefully millions of people, it takes an entire team. One of the most important people on my team has been my copy editor Rodney Rawlings, who streamlined my prose and polished it. Rodney thanks for bringing this book to life.

Finally, I wish to thank Bill Vanderleest for his expertise and professionalism as both a realtor and a property manager. When working on your business it is absolutely imperative that you form relationships based on trust, integrity, and mutual respect. Bill, you have exemplified all these qualities and have become a dear friend in the process. It was your guidance and support that got me to purchase my first multi-family investment property several years ago, and for that I am eternally grateful. I look forward to a long and prosperous business and personal relationship with you for years to come.

Contents

Preface

What is it that enables some people to rise to seemingly unimaginable heights of financial success, while others suffer from lack, poverty, and failure? What keeps some people driving through life toward their destination regardless of obstacles and roadblocks, while others give up at the first sign of trouble? The answer is not as complex as you might first believe. Those who achieve significant levels of financial success make it a habit to follow a few simple disciplines on a daily basis like saving a part of all they earn, reducing their expenses, investing their money with the expectation of a reasonable return and ensuring the safety of their principal.

The Financial Fitness Blueprint is for those serious about changing their lives and walking the road less travelled.

The term **financial fitness** is used a great deal in this book, an analogy with physical fitness, an area that I have been involved with for much of my life. I wrote this book for people who truly desire to become financially independent, to live from the resources of their own creation and write their own paycheque at the end of the day. It is for the individual searching for guidance on avoiding the pitfalls and credit traps that bury so many under a pile of debt.

Most importantly, it is for those still in middle school, high school, or university. It is for you to understand that the habits you develop in your early years will shape your personal philosophy about money and finance, which will have a dramatic impact on whether or not you achieving the financial success available to all who truly seek it.

In reading these pages you will find that the same disciplines that would bring you success in your pursuit of physical health can also be applied to building your financial house. I am sure you wouldn't feel comfortable living in a house with its foundation hastily built. You would want it built with time and detail to attention so it can withstand the strongest storms. If you exercise this discipline and attention to detail in your financial affairs you too can rise to the level of the top 5% in society who have created their lives by design.

This book is primarily a guide that provides concrete steps for those who wish to take charge of their financial future. No matter what line of work you are in, or how much money you make, if you realize that you have a bigger purpose in life and are ready to go after it — if you don't want to settle for less than your absolute best — these pages are written for you.

So where do we begin? If you are in your late teens or older, you know educational systems across the country are failing to adequately prepare citizens to understand how money works. Is this a mere coincidence that, people are sold the idea of going to school and getting a good education so they can get a decent job? Or are we being programmed to become slaves to the system and live in perpetual servitude?

I believe the answer is very clear, so let's take a look at how we have been conditioned by the educational system to suppress our dreams and stifle our own creativity. As students we were told to sit in rows, speak when spoken to, focus on grades, and start planning for our careers. Many of us were told to find a company that offered a pension plan and the company would take care of us and ensure our retirement years would be golden.

Unfortunately that formula for financial success has failed miserably. Today you can no longer rely on your employer. When it comes to your financial success you must have a solid plan of your own to create the life you want to live. Today you need to save more, spend less and invest for your future.

Our schools have preached safety and mediocrity to our students and have done a great job producing workers who embrace a poverty mentality — workers who struggle to make ends meet, who pay the highest taxes as a percentage of their incomes, who seldom have an effective plan for their retirements, and whose only source of income is from their "JOB" (just over broke). Yes, our schools have done a fabulous job preparing us to follow in the footsteps of the masses and live a mediocre life. In doing so they have failed to awaken the entrepreneurial spirit in students and instill the idea that profits are far better than wages for securing one's financial future.

Don't get me wrong, I believe in the value of education and have worked in the system for more than 17 years as both teacher and administrator. It is my love for teaching and educating others that has brought me to this point in my life.

I am in no way saying education is not important. In fact those who pursue postsecondary education are in far better shape to create a solid financial house for their future; statistics clearly support this. In our fast-paced economy, education is absolutely essential for success and those who don't at least complete their high school diploma will be a major drain on government resources and have great difficulty locating suitable employment, let alone achieving financial freedom.

It is absolutely amazing how many people complete their schooling and go through life never understanding the first thing about personal finance. Millions of well-educated adults holding countless degrees from prestigious universities end up broke by the time they retire. If education is indeed the great equalizer, why is our society plagued by millions of educated retirees who made good money during their working years and still end up relying on government handouts?

If we analyzed the question in depth, we could come up with a variety of reasons for the poor financial picture millions find themselves in at the end of their working careers. But a fundamental reason for this travesty is our government's lack of foresight to establish a standard curriculum covering the real value of money and how people can successfully navigate and secure their financial futures.

That said, the anaemic bank accounts held by millions worldwide and their lack of sufficient financial education should not be blamed entirely on their governments or educational systems. As adults we need to shoulder our own responsibility. We cannot continue to hold pity parties about our lack of financial success.

Some might not agree that it is each individual's own responsibility to take steps to secure their own financial future. But I would challenge them to answer the following question: If not you, then who? No one cares about your financial future more than you.

Should you ever find yourself in the unenviable position of having others care more about your financial future than you, take it as a clear indication you are heading down the road to financial disaster. One of the major factors that stop people from truly achieving things in life is that they are continually looking for reasons to explain their lack of success, financial or otherwise. The blame game has never promoted anyone to any great status in life and it never will.

If you want to reap the rewards of this world, you will have to adjust your sails, change your attitude, and take full responsibility for your own future. If you open yourself up to new ideas and commit to taking positive action, I can assure you that the information in this book will be of tremendous value in moving you toward a brighter financial future. You will then be among the minority in society who leave legacies instead of liabilities behind.

The Change

As a young man growing up I was carefree and happy-go-lucky. My thoughts focused on athletics and personal training (two things I was very good at). Rarely did the thought of money ever cross my mind. In fact, I can't recall any of my friends ever discussing money, investments, or planning for the future. To be blatantly honest, I knew nothing and was walking on very thin financial ice.

My lack of money knowledge can be traced back to the fact that we grew up with very little of it in our household. We were not destitute, but with only a 7th-grade education, raising four children on her own, my mom had to focus on survival. Money was desperately lacking, and was never talked about. The only thing I knew was that we didn't have any.

When I was in my early 30s, a good friend posed a simple but profound question to me: "Courtney, what are you doing about your financial future?" To be honest I didn't want to answer. I had never thought about my financial goals. Like so many, I was living paycheque to paycheque and assumed I was doing just fine. At the time I didn't even have an investment account or knew what an RRSP was.

I deflected his question, telling him we would discuss the matter at the end of our workout. Besides, as a serious athlete I hated spending quality workout time talking about anything not related to fitness and training. When the workout was over he asked if I had time for a conversation. I thought about making up an excuse, but decided to put my pride aside and hear what he had to say.

A week later I am in his office discussing the pros and cons of investing in RRSP's. **[A registered retirement savings plan (RRSP) is a savings account that allows a person to defer paying tax on money being saved for retirement. Contribution limits are based on how much you earn and are tax deductible at the time of deposit. An RRSP can contain**

stocks, bonds, mutual funds, GICs, contracts and even mortgage-backed equities].

Robert went on to explain that the duration of your investment horizon and the compounding of interest were the most important factors for financial success. **[Compounding is when your investments generate earnings and those earnings are reinvested to generate their own earnings].** He urged me to get started immediately while also teaching me about the value of home ownership and the importance of leveraging. Up to that point I had been content to live in the moment. I had no plan, I had no role models, and no goals for my future. How was I to succeed?

That day was the beginning of my financial education, and to this day I go to the seminars, read books, and attend classes to increase my financial literacy. So let me ask you the same questions:

- What are you doing about your financial future?
- Do you have a clearly defined plan to achieve success?
- Are you aware of the opportunities surrounding you every day?
- Is your financial blueprint good enough to build a solid foundation that will ensure your financial success?

These are hard questions, and the sooner you can answer them the better off you will be. I suggest that you make this a priority and don't put if off any longer. Thirty is not the age to begin planning for your future success. By that stage of life you should be well on your way. But if you have not started, take comfort in knowing you still have time to set things right. Let my story serve as a warning. The best time to begin was yesterday; the second-best time is today. Putting it off any longer would be a colossal error in judgment.

Take Action Now

Most people fail before they start. I want you to think about that statement. What does it mean? It means the fear of failure for some is so great that it often immobilizes them from taking action. This emotional state leads to procrastination. Many of us can relate to this kind of fear in one way or another. Maybe it has kept you from going after that promotion at work, or stopped you from asking for that date, or prevented you from writing that book you have been dreaming of for years. Maybe it has stopped you from taking action to purchase that piece of real estate that might have gotten you started on the road to your financial freedom.

Yes, fear is real and it can be quite debilitating. However, if you are not willing to take action and face your fears you will continue to live a mediocre life. How much has your inability to act cost you when it comes to your relationships, your health, or your finances? If you are anything like I was in my early years, I am sure it has cost you a great deal.

So what do you do when confronted with this thief of dreams? I want you to remember this statement the next time you consider giving up on your dream:

You don't have to be great to start but you have to start to be great.

It is never too late to begin, but you should know that time can work for or against you. It is rumoured that Albert Einstein said "time and compounding is the eighth wonder of the world and he who understands it, earns it ... he who doesn't ... pays it." I don't know if there is any verifiable way of finding out whether or not Einstein indeed said these words or not. However, what I do know is that by getting started immediately you will be able to leverage the power of time for maximum impact on your financial future. If you continue to put things off you will find that time soon becomes your greatest enemy.

The concepts shared in this book are not new and are in no way my original ideas. They have been used successfully by men and women for generations and continue to reward those who use them today. However, what you will find here is a fresh perspective on the topic of personal finance that is simple and easy to understand regardless of your background.

All I ask is that you read this book all the way through and begin to implement the strategies discussed. Doing so will put you in distinguished company: the top 5% in society who understand that knowledge, coupled with applied action is the great equalizer.

So let's begin by exploring one of the most important factors that will determine whether you reap the financial rewards you seek: the power of your thoughts.

Chapter One

Mindset

The degree to which we allow our minds to be consumed by a thought whether good or bad will impact the decisions we make and the lives we ultimately create.

—Courtney Carroll

I n his classic book *Think and Grow Rich,* Napoleon Hill states countless times that whatever the mind of man can conceive and believe can be achieved. This one profound idea has led men and women from all walks of life to astounding success.

The trouble is people who truly achieve this level of success are the minority, not the majority. It is a sad truth that millions of men and women will see their dreams buried with them because they didn't believe the natural law that governs the universe — that thoughts are truly things.

Born to Win

We are all born to win in the game of life. Unfortunately, many people settle for substandard or average financial fitness because of their own limiting beliefs about money, or because they have allowed other people's opinions of them to become their own realities. Your personal belief about money is probably the most important factor in the achievement of financial success. So whether you believe you can, or believe you can't — you are right!

Wealth must be conceived in the mind first, and then those thoughts must be turned into practical steps to acquire wealth before it can ever happen in reality. Your personal beliefs about money will have a direct impact on your ability to attract it and have it work for you.

To become financially fit we need to look at the events in our lives that have shaped our personal beliefs about money and wealth. If you have doubts about whether you deserve to be financially fit, then stick with me. I will help you move beyond your limiting beliefs and show you how you can create the life you truly deserve.

For most of my teen years and early adulthood my personal outlook about money was largely influenced by my family and the people in my inner circle. Probably the most influential of all was my mother who worked hard to make ends meet, but was never confident that she could attract abundance in her life. My mother finished school in grade seven and worked as a caregiver into her early twenties. Fortunately she was sponsored by a family and moved from Jamaica to Canada to pave a better road for her children. With very little to her name except a fierce determination to survive, she sent for her four children (me being the youngest) to join her.

Our early years in Canada proved very difficult while my mother worked several jobs to make ends meet. We never lacked for food or shelter, but outside of the basics there wasn't room for any extras. Although we didn't have much, my mom told us to be grateful for everything we did have, because we were better off than many others in the world. I must admit, as a young child I didn't get much comfort from that, and neither did my siblings I am sure.

My mom was a hard worker but she was mainly concerned with survival and didn't see the many opportunities for wealth creation all around her. She saw poverty in her life and because of her limited experience wasn't able to create wealth, or accumulate any kind of savings for her retirement.

For many years I shared my mom's limiting beliefs about wealth creation, because I was exposed to her fears every day. Everything I bought was met with the question of how much it cost. It didn't matter what the item was, my mom would tell me it was too expensive and I could have bought it cheaper somewhere else. She was always telling me we couldn't afford this or that. Little did she know the influence those messages would have on my outlook about money. For years I felt guilty about spending money.

The fact that every adult in my family had the same opinions and outlook as my mom was clearly evident, as not one member of my family had achieved financial fitness. They were all coasting through life hoping and praying things would work out. They didn't have a plan for success, nor the belief that it was achievable.

I often went to bed wondering what would happen if my mom lost her job. I would lie awake worrying about my mother not having enough for us to survive. This came from us constantly moving from one apartment building to the next and having to live in Ontario Provincial housing complexes. It felt like we were always on the run; we had moved four times, and I attended five different elementary schools in the first five years of moving to Canada. Where were the opportunities that were promised when we decided to migrate from our home in Jamaica to seek a better life in Canada?

The Right Connections

In my late teens and early 20s, my circle of friends changed dramatically. I was a university graduate and surrounded myself with individuals who wanted more from life. We all had dreams of landing a good job and getting a paycheque that would allow us to live better than our parents. But even at this stage of life I still felt I shouldn't dream too big or wish for too much. I grew up hearing the message that money was evil and therefore I was content with just getting enough to support my family and buy a few luxuries that I wasn't able to afford when I was younger.

I was a hard worker and often worked overtime to earn extra cash. But my efforts were useless, because I still didn't understand the laws of money. I had no savings, and my investment portfolio was nonexistent. I feared not having enough money, but couldn't stop myself from spending what I made, or giving it to family members who knew nothing of how to attract and keep money in their lives.

In my early years of working I earned a significant amount of money, but my lack of understanding about how ones mindset shapes their personal philosophy, caused me to squander the very thing I wanted to attract.

To make matters worse, although my closest friends and I had dreams of elevating our lives, no one had any idea on how to create wealth. They were as lost as I was and were mainly concerned with saving a few dollars every week so they would have spending money for the clubs on the weekends. At times it seemed their biggest goals were chasing girls and drinking.

Nurturing our Dreams

I have a question. Why do most people settle for what life gives them, rather than demanding from life what they really want? It's been said that we are all born with the seeds of greatness and engineered for success. So why do millions of people put the brakes on their dreams after leaving grade school?

Could it be that our dreams were crushed at an early age by the very people who were supposed to be our biggest advocates? If we take a closer look, we might shed some light on the matter. Think back to your early childhood and the unlimited potential that welled up inside you. You were invincible. You had mighty dreams of conquering the world and amassing fortunes. You had an unshakable belief in what you would accomplish with your life, and nothing was going to stand in your way.

You couldn't wait for your first day of school to share your dreams with the new friends you would meet.

Unfortunately for many, this is where their dreams started to die. At first it was easy to ignore the negative comments of a few friends. But as time passed they heard their goals dismissed, not only by other children, but also by adults. Teachers and even some parents would tell them they didn't have the needed skills to be successful in one field or another.

Seemingly innocent comments like these have had a terrible impact on millions of students worldwide. I have seen the hurt and disappointment when a child is told by a teacher that he or she could never become a doctor or a lawyer. When people in positions of power impose their biased opinions on innocent children, the result is self-doubt and low self-esteem.

No one has the right to determine what we are each capable of, but children or young adults can't see this very clearly. A negative feedback loop is reinforced every time they are told they can't achieve great things, until eventually their mind springs into action giving them exactly what they believe.

Thinking Wealthy

For years my own limiting beliefs prevented me from attracting wealth and abundance into my life. I was following the misguided direction of family and community members who did not know the secrets to wealth.

Unless we step outside of our comfort zones to learn from others who have moved their lives to the next level, we will remain slaves to the system, taking what life gives us, instead of demanding what we truly want.

This mistake keeps millions trapped in permanent servitude, wandering through life without the will to live up to their potential.

The years of limiting beliefs instilled in me were hard to overcome, even as an adult. It took consistent and determined action to surround myself with people who saw things, not as they were, but how they could be, before I could begin changing my thought patterns. Eventually I was able to override the effect of my upbringing in order to put my life on the right track.

Do you have such limiting beliefs stopping you from living your life by design?

Are you following a script laid out by someone else about how to live? Or are you co-creating a life of abundance, joy, and accomplishment?

Truth be told, everything you have in your life to this point is of your own creation. The house you currently own, or apartment you are renting, is a result of the values and beliefs you have had up to this point. So is the car you drive, the work you are employed in, and even the salary you are earning. You might find this hard to believe, but it is absolutely true. If you have nothing in the bank and nothing saved for retirement, you are in this position by choice.

But here is the good news. If you are not happy with the results you are currently experiencing, guess what? You don't have to accept them, you can change them.

Life will give you what you desire as long as you can clearly define what it is you want. Once you have made the decision to attract something in your life, you must maintain focus until it is achieved. Think **FOCUS: Firmly On Course Until Successful**. This means you have to commit to the task at hand and apply a persistent mental attitude towards achieving your goal.

Habits of the Rich

There is a definite distinction between the habits of those who are rich and those who are poor. The rich have made the study of wealth part of their life's mission, and they imitate the habits of others who have amassed fortunes. The formula for creating wealth is there for anyone curious enough to pick up the right books and read through the pages of history. The same basic principles and habits that created wealth for others are available to you.

Many people believe that the rich will continue to get richer and the poor will continue to be poor, and I can't say I disagree. Some would go as far as blaming the rich for the poor man's position in life, claiming that there isn't enough wealth to go around. Well, if you are among those who blame the rich, I suggest you stop and put your energy to more productive use. Blaming the rich will not get you anywhere, and by doing so you are preventing yourself from ever becoming rich. You can't go around despising the very thing you wish to attract into your life. Besides, doing so would make you a big hypocrite.

I would even go so far as to tell you that you need to admire those who have created wealth and do your best to copy them. The difference between those who accumulate wealth and those who don't is basically their awareness. Those who have achieved financial freedom understand the game of money and have learned how to make sure they are on the winning side at the end of the game.

Those who struggle through life never take the time to learn the rules of the game. These people often live their lives as spectators, never getting off the bench to contribute to the outcome of the game. They willingly accept what life gives them, and for that reason should not complain about their meager returns at the end of the day.

Those who succeed financially want the ball at the most critical time of the game, because they want to be totally responsible for the game's outcome.

The Rules of Money

Over the years I have learned to work, not harder, but smarter — which provides a much better return. I have learned to follow the rules of money laid down by those who have gone down this path before. I will share these rules with you in the hope you will adopt them and put your financial affairs in order.

- **Rule number one.** *Pay yourself first!* Money comes quickly and easily to the person who commits to putting aside a minimum of 1/10 of their earnings for future wealth. The more money you put away, the more you will be able to attract into your life. So develop the habit of saving at least 10% of what you earn.
- **Rule number two.** *Reduce your expenses!* If you are going to win the money game, you must reduce your expenses and live on no more than 90% of your monthly earnings. If you adopt this rule early enough in your life you should be able to retire

in comfort. For those who want to ensure financial security, I would suggest living on no more than 80% of what you earn. This will ensure that you will have at least 20% of your income to grow your wealth. For those looking to make a significant impact on society, living on 75% of their income and donating 5% to bless others will bring huge rewards.

- **Rule number three.** *Put your money to work!* Money does not eat, drink, sleep, or get tired. It is a willing slave that will work tirelessly for you. You will find your money doubles over time if invested properly. So find suitable employment for your cash so it can work at making you more money.

- **Rule number four.** *Protect your money!* Invest in businesses you are familiar with. I have heard it said that the truly wealthy hate to lose money. That should be the case for everyone, regardless of financial position, but unfortunately it is not. Your money will stay in your control if you are careful how it's handled. Capital preservation is more important than the hope of capital appreciation. A wise man will do his homework and take advice from those who have successfully managed their own finances in order not to jeopardize his capital. He will learn about a particular business by surrounding himself with people knowledgeable in that field and skilled in the handling of money. Protect your hard-earned dollars by knowing your business.

- **Rule number five.** *Singles are better than home runs!* Don't chase fancy investments that promise unrealistic returns on your money. Exercise caution, and remember that wealth is created over time — there is no magic pill. There are lots of tricksters plotting to take your money. So look for reasonable and consistent gains on your money over time, because in this ball game singles are better than home runs.

I've outlined the steps that have been used by millions before you to accumulate wealth and win the money game. The rest is up to you. You can ignore the teachings in this book and continue to live life as a spectator, or you can start working on a bright financial future. Remember our smart choices will accompany us through our lives and serve to remind us of our journey. Our foolish acts will also accompany us, but the memories they leave are often bitter and laced with regret.

Taking Stock

Before we go any further I want you to take a few minutes to reflect on the questions below. I would suggest that you use a journal to record your answers, as this will allow you to see where changes are needed, when analyzing your personal philosophy about money.

- Have you laid out a personal plan for achieving financial success?
- What does that plan look like? Do you have an income goal in mind, a cash-flow target, or net-worth amount you wish to achieve? Write it down!
- Are you living the life you've dreamed of? Or the one you have settled for?
- If you have not created your life by design, whose plans are you following, and why?
- Have you allowed other people's negative comments to cripple your imagination and stop you from laying a foundation for your financial success?
- Do you blame others for your current financial position, or have you taken total responsibility for where you are today?

Your answers will give you clues about your personal philosophy. It's important that you spend a few minutes to accurately reflect on these answers before moving on. As with most things in life, progress comes when we know where we are starting from.

So have you settled — or are you charting your own course? An easy way to find out is to take a close look at your finances. The consequences of your personal outlook about money cannot be disputed and will show up there. Your bank account, although not the only indicator of success, will reveal the effects of your personal philosophy.

So let's start our journey together and develop a financial fitness program. Step one, as we have seen, is to lay the foundation for success by practising the habit of saving.

Chapter Two

The Saving Habit

Since the collapse of the global financial markets of 2007/08, and with current stock market volatility showing no signs of easing, many Canadians are wondering if they will have enough money to survive their retirements. It's a good question, and the answer will prove quite sobering for many people. I am amazed at just how many adults live for the moment with very little regard for their financial future. The "got to have it now" mentality and the inability to delay gratification have proven costly for millions now grappling with a bleak financial future.

The current level of uncertainty facing the European market at the beginning of 2012 is even more alarming. A potential default of Greece, Italy, Spain, or Portugal would have a ripple effect on all economies that would take years, if not decades, for individual investors and many countries to overcome.

What impact will this have on people around the world living on fixed incomes as the price of goods soar even further out of control? What about those on social assistance, what will happen when governments reduce or eliminate program funding in order to balance their budgets and reduce their deficits?

Don't think it's possible? The Harper government is in the middle of an ongoing strategic operating review, searching for $1 billion in cuts for 2012, $2 billion for 2013/14, and $4 billion by 2014/15. Nearly 70 government departments and agencies have been required to submit scenarios for a

5% and 10% cut to their budgets[1]. This means thousands of people will lose their jobs over the next several years. We have witnessed the increased tension and unrest this has caused between Toronto's Mayor Rob Ford and the various government sectors forced to trim their budgets by 10%[2]. The question that remains to be answered is: What will be the fate of those who lose their jobs because of the proposed cuts?

People living on government assistance or a fixed income can expect a very tough future. If the European Union goes into default, the banking sector could find itself in a freefall while governments will be forced to stimulate their economies by printing more money and slashing services. For those who are relying on Old Age Security and CPP, I would tell them to think again. We are in for a wild ride, and millions of retirees will be unprepared to survive what is supposed to be the best years of their lives. We have to wake up and accept the fact that things are changing and that our governments will not be able to do everything for much longer. It will be up to each individual to secure his or her own financial future.

What does this mean? Well, if you haven't developed the habit of saving and haven't invested your money wisely, you could be in serious trouble. I don't want to be an alarmist, but we need to start looking more deeply into every move made by governments, not just in this country, but globally. We can't continue to bury our heads in the sand and hope the future will work out. Hope without a plan is futile. Fortunately, this book provides a blueprint that is time-tested, is easy to implement, and gets results.

Lost Decades of Saving

For the last two decades, national savings levels have decreased from 20% to less than 4% in Canada[3] and even lower in the United States. As a consumer-driven society we are constantly on the lookout for the next big sale and have been content living paycheque to paycheque. If nothing else,

---

1   Lilley, Brian. Sun Media, "Lilley's Pad." Last modified 03/02/2012. Accessed March 15, 2012. http://blogs.canoe.ca/lilleyspad/category/government-debt/.

2   Doolittle, Robyn. Thestar.com, "Police board demands 10% cuts." Last modified 10/05/11. Accessed 12/22/11. http://www.thestar.com/news/crime/article/1065089--police-board-demands-10-budget-cut.

3   Cockburn, Carrie. The Globe and Mail, "The steep decline in Canadian and US household savings rate." Last modified 02/03/12. Accessed April 15, 2012. http://www.theglobeandmail.com/globe-investor/personal-finance/the-steep-decline-in-canadian-and-us-household-savings-rates/article2326372/page4/.

the recession of 2007/2008 finally got many Canadians and Americans paying closer attention to how they spend their money. We are seeing an increase in the number of Canadians paying themselves first before satisfying consumer debts. Although the current 5% annual savings rate pales in comparison to the 20% seen a few decades ago, I think it is a move in the right direction.

The concept of paying yourself first is not new. For years it has been used successfully by people disciplined enough to stay the course to amass incredible fortunes.

Unlike North Americans, the Chinese have it right when it comes to saving their money. Chinese government restricts its people to one child to curb population growth, forcing many of their citizens to develop a healthy appetite for saving. This habit resulted in a national savings rate nearing 30% in 2005.[4] Is it any wonder that China appears set to be the country to lead the world out of this economic downturn?

Born to be Rich

> *Rich and poor have this in common: The LORD is the Maker of them all.*
>
> —Proverbs 22:2

This book is not a discussion about religion, but I will refer to a few quotes from one of the greatest books ever written, to illustrate a few points about wealth and poverty.

I grew up in the church listening to the teachings of the Bible. I didn't understand everything, but I do recall hearing clearly that "The love of money is the root of all evil" — which means you cannot put money before God or your family, because to do so would be a sin. I strongly agree with this; the man who puts money first is destined for destruction. God must be in the details of what you are doing.

Unfortunately, many have misinterpreted this scripture to read that money, as opposed to the love of it, is the root of all evil. Nothing could be further from the truth. God wants you to be rich. In Jeremiah 29:11, God speaks to his disciples by saying the following: "I know the plans I have for you, plans to prosper you and not to harm you, and plans to give

---

4   Chamon, Marcos, Kai Lui, and Eswar Prasad. Voxeu.org, "The puzzle of China's household savings rate." Last modified 01/18/11. Accessed 11/22/11. http://www. voxeu.org/index.php?q=node/6028.

you hope and a future."[5] My interpretation is that we were put here to succeed, but misunderstanding of this passage in the Bible has led many to adopt a poverty mentality, never aspiring to rise to any prominent station in life. They believe that denying themselves the pleasures of this earth and settling for what life gives them will get them closer to their spiritual father. This is a destructive idea that will lead you to poverty and being broke and embarrassed at the age of 65.

So if God makes both the rich and the poor, would it not be better to create a financially fit future? Of course it would; we were put here to prosper and make a difference, not to live in constant worry about our finances. Would it not benefit society if you created abundance in all aspects of your life so you could bless those unable to create for themselves? Of course it would; one of the greatest virtues of man is a willingness to lend a hand to people who are down on their luck. Those who can bless others with their gifting will lack for nothing. I will have more to say about the importance of charity later on.

I believe we are all born with the potential to achieve anything we truly want in life. The only limits are those we put on ourselves. Remove those barriers stuck in our subconscious and we quickly realize that everything is possible. Those who understand the unlimited potential of man, and are committed to making an impact on this world, have always found a way to realize their life's purpose. Today we are at the starting point that will help you unleash your unlimited potential.

Pay yourself first

The savings habit is the most important principle of wealth creation. Most people take this fundamental principle for granted and never develop the habit. If you are serious about creating wealth you cannot overlook the importance of saving.

When people hear about the habit of saving, or paying oneself first, they think only about the dollar amount that needs to be set aside each month. Yes, the dollar amount is important. But there is something that happens when you learn this habit which is far more significant than the dollars you accumulate. For years I followed other people's script when it came to my financial fitness. Despite receiving regular raises and earning an above-average income I was living from paycheque to paycheque, saving

---

5 Biblegateway.com, "Jeremiah 29:11 (New International Version)." Accessed 12/08/11. http://www.biblegateway.com/passage/?search=Jeremiah 29:11&version=NIV.

nothing. How could this be? It was very simple. I was following the crowd. But the problem with that is you lose perspective and often can't see where you're headed until it is too late.

There is a saying that when the student is ready the teacher will appear, and I guess I must have been ready. Ready not only to hear the question, but to reflect on it and evaluate where I was and what I was going to do to change my direction. With my friend's help I created a savings plan and started putting a part of all I earned into safe keeping for future investments. Within two years of making a commitment to develop the saving habit I was able to purchase my first home.

This was a monumental moment, as I was the first in my family to purchase my own home. What was impressive was the short time it took me to achieve my goal of home ownership once the goal was clearly laid out and a plan put into place.

For the first 33 years of my life I moved aimlessly about without any plan for my future, operating on the wrong philosophy. I was getting nowhere and was not even aware that I was digging my own grave with the errors in judgment I was making. By changing my outlook, adopting a positive attitude, and developing the habit of saving, I was able to significantly change the direction of my life, and so can you.

Saving Pays

History has shown that men and women who truly understand this principle of saving always find themselves surrounded with opportunities for creating wealth. Some of you might be asking yourselves, "What is so magical about the saving habit?" For starters, it allows you to demonstrate to others that you can be trusted with money.

If you wanted to buy a $300,000 house would you wait until you had the entire amount saved up? No you wouldn't, you would borrow 90% of the value from the bank in order to make that purchase. This means you would have to demonstrate to the bank that you had the discipline needed to save 10% for the down payment. Would the bank have given you a mortgage if you hadn't shown your ability to save a part of the purchase price? Of course not: once the universe is aware of your disciplined habits and respect for money, the floodgates will open, bringing you more than you ever thought possible.

Think about this: The average person works 40 hours a week for 40 years hoping to get a pension for their retirement. Many of these workers live their lives by default and never set goals. For some, the habit of saving is as strange as speaking Urdu — they never learn to do it. After 40-hour weeks and 40 years of labour they find themselves broke and embarrassed at the age of 65. They never took the time to look at the simple mistakes in their outlook and how it would impact their lives.

If you are serious about navigating the new financial realities facing us, you must become the architect of your own plan. You must begin the habit of saving part of all you earn so that you can be trusted with more. Having more allows you to take advantage of the opportunities around you in order to grow your wealth.

Your blueprint for wealth must be clearly visualized in your own mind. You cannot leave it to chance or to someone else to put your plan together. Most people fail to plan and that is precisely why most people fail. Don't let complacency keep you rooted in poverty. Decide today to create more so you can bless others.

It was concerns about my family's finances that spurred me to getting my mutual funds and life insurance licenses. Once I had my licenses it became my mission to educate others so they would avoid the mistakes I made with my money. But little did I know that the very group of people who needed the most help would be the most resistant.

This used to frustrate me but not anymore. I was attending a Les Brown seminar where he said a couple things that changed the way I looked at my prospective clients: "Life is too short trying to change people and convince them about financial independence; if they can't see the picture, move on." "You can't change everyone. It is a full-time job working to change your own life."

You Need to Become a Saver

I want you to think for a minute about the amount of money that has already passed through your hands during your lifetime. For some of you it will be tens of thousands of dollars, for some it will be hundreds of thousands, and for still others it will be millions. The dollar value that you have personally attracted to this point is a reflection of your understanding of how money works in combination with the perceived value you are currently bringing to the market place.

Money is attracted to those who create value in the marketplace. If you are earning $40,000 a year, it might be because the value you bring to the marketplace is not seen to be as great as the value brought by someone making $250,000 per year. However, regardless of the amount you are currently making, there is room for much more if you are willing to follow the principles.

The first thing needed from your end is to adopt this basic principle: Pay yourself first! You work hard and even before you get paid there are a lot of demands on your money. Your mortgage or rent, your car payment, your gym membership, and your grocery and utility bills are just a few, not to mention what your government takes before you even see a dollar. It's no surprise then to find that many people feel they have nothing left to put toward saving for the long run. But unless this habit is changed, these people will find themselves long on retirement years and short on finances.

If you are going to succeed financially, you must put your long-term savings at the top of your priority list. Over the years I have sat with many people who told me they couldn't afford to put money aside, because they had too many bills to pay and couldn't find the extra funds. The truth is; you will always have bills to pay. Understand that you must save and reduce your debts simultaneously if you are to build a financially fit future.

When I worked as a personal trainer I would get questions from my clients about how to get into optimal shape. My answer was that they needed to get into the gym on a regular basis. For me "regular" meant four or five times a week. I would tell them that this might be difficult in the beginning but if they stuck with it and disciplined themselves it would become a habit, like brushing their teeth. With a regular, balanced program the results would come in time.

In addition, I told them they would have to make changes to their eating habits, especially in the amount of calories they consumed. If you are going to the gym regularly, but continue to eat a high junk-food diet, you are going to sabotage the very thing you wish to achieve.

What does physical fitness have to do with financial fitness? For starters, what you learned from a good fitness plan can be applied to your financial plan. The principles for success are almost identical. The person who wants to improve their personal health must reduce the bad debt (the amount of junk food and calories they consume), while increasing their investments (time in the gym training) in order to succeed.

Your financial fitness mirrors the exact habits needed for success in your physical fitness. You have to reduce your expenses (cut out the fat, so to speak) and increase your savings (the meat and potatoes) if you want to build a financially secure foundation for success. You cannot make real progress if you do one thing and neglect the other. They are opposite sides of the same coin. By reducing your expenses and saving simultaneously you will be well on your way to reaping the rich rewards that can only be claimed through the compound effects of a disciplined approach over time.

Roger's Story

I met Roger shortly after his mother passed away from cardiovascular disease. He was referred to me by his cousin. Roger and I had a great meeting while we discussed his financial goals and his insurance needs. Roger had just inherited his mother's house and felt it was important to get life insurance to at least cover the cost of the outstanding mortgage on the house and to start putting a portion of his income into segregated funds for his retirement.

Roger was making good money and felt the extra payments would be easily handled. However, after drawing up the insurance documents Roger decided to put the brakes on the investments. His reasoning was he had too many debts and wanted to pay them off first. I explained to Roger that he needed to commit a portion of what he earned towards savings and investments and use the rest of his earnings to satisfy his debts and living expenses. If he did this he would be able to create a sizable investment over the years.

Roger didn't change his mind, and three years later, despite repeated attempts to get him to see the light he has put no money away for his future. Roger is now in his early 30s and there is still hope for him, but we need to remember habits are too light to be felt until they are too heavy to be broken. Hopefully Roger will be able to change his destructive habits in time.

Here is another example of why you can't put off investing until your debts have been cleared. Imagine having a 25-year mortgage and making the decision that you cannot afford to invest any money into your future until your mortgage is completely paid off. You are now 25 years into the future, and, yes, you are mortgage-free, but you have missed 25 years of the magic of compounding that you will never be able to recoup. You have equity in your home, and that is a good thing; but to gain access to it, you would need to either sell your house or take out a loan against it. This is why you must start saving immediately while reducing your debt.

"When is *now* a good time to begin?" Isn't that a most profound question? It is found on the cover page of one of my favourite books, *Harmonic Wealth* by James Arthur Ray. I find it relevant to include in this chapter because if you get the significance and are willing to change immediately, you will be able to accomplish incredible things. So what clues can we take from those who have amassed stupendous wealth? When we look closely, we realize that the first clue is to begin immediately. Warren Buffet bought his first stock when he was only 11 years old. He purchased six shares of Cities Service at $38.00 per share for himself and his older sister. Buffet sold the stock shortly after for $40.00 and came to regret his mistake as the stock shot up to $200.00 per share[6]. This experience taught him one of the most important lessons of investing: Patience is a virtue.

Buffet, as most of you already know, has gone on to become one of the three richest men in the world, amassing a cool fortune of approximately $60 billion. Yes I said *billion* with a B, not *million* with an M. When interviewed about investing and what mistakes he has made, Mr. Buffet responded that he wished he had started earlier. If the Oracle of Omaha felt age 11 was too late to start investing, what about you?

Some of you might be thinking that Warren Buffet's example is unrealistic, and I would have to agree with you. However, the point I am trying to make should not be lost in this example: You must begin immediately.

I have discussed the topic of personal finance and the importance of setting goals with many clients. Many are on their way to improving their financial outlook, but others have resisted my advice and continue to put savings and investments on the back burner, using the excuse that they have too many bills and can't afford to put any money away. But the debts will always be there. To wait until they are completely paid off is an exercise in futility. These individuals are looking at life through a poverty lens and cannot see the abundance flowing around them.

How Much Should You Save?

When I was growing up, I was under the impression that only the wealthy got wealthy and the poor stayed poor. As I got older I realized that the wealthy created more wealth because they understood the rules

---

6 "Warren Buffett," Biography.com, http://www.biography.com/people/warren-buffett-9230729 (accessed Jan 05, 2012).

of money and applied them diligently to their daily lives. There is a misunderstanding that if you don't make above-average income you cannot achieve financial fitness. This is an absolute lie because I have seen firsthand what can happen when individuals make changes in their personal outlook and commit themselves to their financial goals.

Whether you earn minimum wage, earn the national average, or are in the top 5% of income earners, the rules for wealth are the same. You must begin by committing a part of all you earn to savings. It is not what you earn it is what you keep that creates wealth. The person earning minimum wage but putting money away toward future wealth will find themselves in a better financial position than the person making the national average in income but investing nothing toward their future. The question that many are asking is how much should they save.

The amount you save will depend on the amount of disposable income you have after meeting your monthly financial obligations. [**Disposable income is the amount of money remaining after taxes, bills, rent, mortgage, and other living expenses have been subtracted from your pay**]. The reason we use disposable income as our starting point rather than total income, is to show that high income earners may actually have less disposable income than average income earners. One reason is that, as their income increases, many people take on more debt and higher bills, reducing the amount of disposable income available.

Let me explain. When I bought my first house I couldn't stay in Toronto, because house prices were way beyond my means. So I looked at the city of Scarborough, only to find that I still couldn't afford what I wanted. So I kept looking east and eventually I was able to settle on a property that cost me $202,000 in Whitby, Ontario.

The house was a four-level back split, and after converting the basement into a beautiful living space I sold the property for a small profit and moved to Scarborough after only ten months and took on a higher mortgage. Although my income had gone up, I was now paying more of that income to service a $275,000 mortgage. I have since sold that home to buy a bigger house with an even bigger mortgage. Fortunately, I am now in a position to handle the increased expenses, but what would have happened if I stayed in the first house or even the second? Answer — I would no longer have any mortgage payments to worry about. The more you can do to reduce your debts, the more money you will have working for you to create financial freedom.

It is a natural part of life to want more as your income grows, but you must guard against this, especially if you do not understand how money works. Failing to pay attention to this warning could leave you in a world of financial hurt in the future.

So how much should you save? Those who are committed to creating a financially fit future have traditionally put aside 15% to 20% of their annual income.

I can already hear you saying, "I don't make $100,000, and if I did I probably wouldn't be reading this book about getting my financial fitness in order." First of all, the amount of money you make has nothing at all to do with your level of financial knowledge. Many of the top 5% income earners are struggling to keep afloat, simply because they have bitten off way more than they can chew and have never stopped to put a financial blueprint together. Second, we need to be clear that regardless of the amount you make, we are asking you to commit a *percentage*, not a specific dollar amount. Saving 15% to 20% of what you make regardless of whether it is $100,000 or $40,000 is not always easy, but if you are willing to apply the discipline and commit to this kind of saving you will not be short of money later.

So what about the average worker who is just barely getting by? What amount should he commit to wealth creation? I would say at minimum 10%. For many, this will prove difficult, and I can understand that. But if you do what is hard, your life will be easy.

"But my expenses are way too high, how could I do this?" If your expenses are already out of control and you cannot for the life of you come up with 10%, don't give up. What you need to do is start with whatever amount you can reasonably part with. If that is only 2%, then that is where you will need to start. The key to any form of success is taking the first step.

If you are making $2,000 a month after taxes you might find it hard to sacrifice and commit $200.00 toward your savings. But what if you decided to gradually increase the percentage you contribute toward savings from month to month? What if we started by putting away 2% in the first month — that is, the equivalent of $40 — for your future wealth? It isn't much I agree, but it is a start, and that is the point. Starting with 2% instead of 10% is easier on the wallet and the psyche, and it allows you time to look for ways of cutting out wasteful expenses.

Some of you might be thinking that with only $2,000 there could not possibly be room for wasteful spending. However, you would be surprised at what some of your daily habits and mistakes in financial judgment are costing you.

To continue with our example above, you decide to put 3% toward your savings in month number two ($60) and feel totally alive and empowered, because you have put $100.00 toward your future that you didn't think was possible a few months ago. Bolstered by this new power, you commit 4% in month number three ($80) and find yourself addicted to saving and looking for more and more ways to save.

After 10 months you have now reached 10%. More importantly, you realize that this was possible all along, and that you just needed a process to get you started. You do a quick calculation and realize that even though you only bring home $2,000 after taxes, you have already accumulated $1,280 toward your future. Best of all, there was no pain — you didn't need to make drastic changes in your lifestyle to accomplish this. You realize that your future is more important than all the debts you owe and you have made it a priority to pay yourself a part of everything you earn before satisfying any other obligations. Congratulations! You are on the right track.

Make Time Work for You

Putting 10% away each year is easy to do, but it is also easy not to do, and not doing it doesn't actually leave you broke at the end of the day, the week, or even a year. But the compound effect of this error in judgment repeated for 20 to 30 years leads to financial disaster.

The opposite of disaster is financial success and the ability to live a good life. Those who are willing to follow a few simple rules, like reducing spending and saving a part of all they earn, will meet with untold financial success at the end of the day. Successful people understand that following a few simple rules every day doesn't lead to immediate success. They understand that there must be a cultivation period before the magic of life yields a bountiful harvest. Just like the farmer who plants in the spring and reaps in the fall, those who achieve success exhibit patience and discipline, never taking their eyes off the prize. Successful people don't see things as they are, they see things for what they could be, and it is this that separates them from those who fail.

Your outlook is the key to unlocking the treasures you were born to possess. When you have the right outlook you will stop looking for instant gratification. You will start to see the bigger picture and your bigger purpose instead of dwelling only on what is visible to the naked eye. With the right outlook you will no longer look for immediate changes tomorrow, next week, or next month. You will operate from a place of total confidence, knowing that the compound effects of investing a part of all you earn and weighing before you pay, for 20 to 30 years, will lay the foundation for a fit financial future. There is no secret to financial success beyond: you are either doing or not doing. Make sure you are doing all you can to take charge of your life.

The Cost of Retirement

How much will you need to retire? This is a very difficult question to answer. How much you need will depend on a number of factors that are unique for everyone. If you plan to live a simple life during your retirement, not travel, entertain, or spend much money on leisure and eating out, your needs might not be much. However, if you plan on travelling, living in a new home, enjoying recreational activities, and entertaining friends, then your needs will be much greater.

Here is my question to you. If you have devoted all of your best years to working and providing for your family, shouldn't your retirement years be the most rewarding time of your life? Isn't this the time when we get to eat our dessert first, sip champagne on the beach, and watch the sunrises and the sunsets over the horizon?

I believe you would agree that after 30 to 40 years (and for some unfortunate people, 40 to 50 years) of servitude in the workforce, we should be able to retire in comfort. The sad truth is that many people will retire to a life of poverty. But this doesn't have to be your fate; you can set your sails for a brighter retirement. But you must become captain of your own ship.

There is now overwhelming evidence to support the importance of saving more, spending less and investing for your future. In November 2011 a report called *90+ in the United States: 2006 – 2008* was released by the U.S Department of Commerce[7]. Written by Wan He and Mark N. Muenchrath, the report highlighted that the fastest-growing segment of the U.S. population was people over 90. The study showed that from 1980 to 2010 the 90-and-older population had steadily increased. This trend is expected to continue into the middle of the century. There were 720,000 people over 90 in 1980 and more than 1.9 million in 2010. The total

---

7   He, Wan, and Mark Muenchrath. American Community Survey Report, "90 in the United States: 2006 -2008." Last modified Nov, 2011. Accessed 11/27/2011. http://www.census.gov/prod/2011pubs/acs-17.pdf. \

population aged 90 and over is projected to more than quadruple from 2010 to 2050, compared to a doubling of the population aged 65 to 89.

With new medical breakthroughs and a push for healthier lifestyles, we can only expect the standard of living to continually increase and life expectancy to keep on rising. This means that unless we put significant money aside for our retirements there is a good chance we will outlive our money. So we need to get serious about our financial house and build a foundation that will withstand the storms ahead.

So how much will you need to retire? Only you can be the judge of that. For me I have not set any limits. My goal is to keep on earning and investing for as long as I can in order to protect my family and be able to have my dessert and eat it during my retirement years.

How to Get $500,000 for Your Retirement

What if you needed to save half a million dollars to live the life you envisioned throughout your retirement? Could you do it? If you have the right mindset, invest appropriately and begin early, it should be easily within your grasp.

Some of you might be thinking $500,000 is not realistic from where you currently sit. If that is what you are thinking, chances are there are still errors in your outlook preventing you from seeing what is possible.

Others might be thinking $500,000 is too small a goal for the retirement lifestyle they have in mind. Like you, I understand that there are no real limits to what we can achieve financially if we operate with the right philosophy. However, this is only an example and nothing more. The size of your goals will determine the strength of your commitment and drive to achieve it. So go ahead, aim high!

So your goal is to have $500,000 by age 65. How do you get there? Well, if you are in your teens and reading this, good for you. You have the power of time and compounding on your side. And despite what is currently happening in our financial markets you can position yourself very nicely in order to achieve your financial goals. But let's say you want to wait until you finish university or college before you begin your retirement savings plan. How much will you need to put away to achieve your goal?

Today the average student completes college or university around the age of 22. Let's imagine that like me you took a victory lap and stayed at it for one extra year before you decided to test your worth in the real world. So now you are 23 or 24 years old looking to land that high paying job you were promised during your university years. You finally secure a job, not in your field of study, but you are good with it because you can start paying off that dreaded student loan.

You are now 25 years old and have developed some good habits along the way. You decide that paying yourself $25.00 a week or $100.00 a month is a smart thing to do to ensure your financial success. You reason that if you continued to do this for the next 40 years of your working life you should be able to retire with at least $500,000.

Let's take a look and see if you are right. If you were able to invest your money at a 10 percent interest compounded for 40 years, you would surpass your goals. In fact, you would have more than $600,000 saved and all it would have cost you is $100.00 a month.

But what if, like so many 25 year olds, you fell victim to living for the moment and were just too busy hanging with your friends and spending your money foolishly during your twenties? You finally get serious at age 35 and realize you have made some major errors in your financial life. You want to correct things and get back to that old goal of $500,000. Only trouble is, you don't know how much you will need to save every month in order to achieve this goal. You have wasted 10 years and have nothing to show for it.

After consulting with a financial coach you realize that it will take you $653.00 a month to reach your goal (assuming a 10% rate of return). Your inability to get started on your plan at age 25 has created a situation that is almost impossible to achieve. How are you going to do this? The increased savings required would be 6.5 times more than what you would need had you started saving at age 25. If you haven't started on your plan, you need to consider the following question: When is *now* a good time to begin?

Late to the Party

If the example above isn't sobering enough for you, let's take a look at the cost of lost opportunity. What impact would a regular investment of $100.00 a month at 10% have on your future wealth? More importantly, what is the opportunity cost when the saving habit is not adopted at an early age? Let's take a closer look at how money works, and why you need to get it right.

If you were to start consistently putting aside $100.00 a month at age 25 you would save a grand total of $637,680 by the age of 65. Isn't that incredible?

And yet, did you know that that $100.00 a month equals total cash of only $48,000? That's right; you only put $48,000 into the pot. It was the magic of time and compounding investment returns that brought you a return of 13.29 times your money!

Aren't you excited by the possibilities? You should be. There is no magic here, just simple mathematics, and I can guarantee that if you get it and get it early, there is no limit to what you can achieve in your financial life. Others have done it, and millions around the world continue to reap the benefits when they practise a few simple habits on a daily basis.

Suppose you didn't pick up this book at 25, perhaps you didn't believe wealth was possible for you, or felt you had all the time in the world. Suppose it took your friends one extra year to convince you of the idea of putting together a financial fitness blueprint. Not a big deal, right? After all, it is only one year. I mean, what would be the big deal if you invested for 39 years and your friend invested for 40?

Well, the truth is, it makes a world of difference to your bottom line. Simply putting off what you know to be the critical step could end up costing you $61,590, because you started one year later. Are you willing to forfeit that kind of money when all that is needed is for you to start developing the habit of putting aside $100.00 a month for one extra year? I certainly hope your answer is an emphatic no!

The opportunity cost becomes more extreme the longer you continue to make money mistakes. If you started saving $100.00 a month at age 30 instead of age 25, you will have $382,830 by the age of 65. To be honest, the majority of people would be happy with a treasure chest of $382,830 when they retire. Many who wish to live a simple life during their retirements might have no difficulty surviving with a nest egg like this socked away.

The unfortunate reality is that the majority of Canadians won't even come close to having this much invested for their financial future. Only a very small minority of the Canadian population are forward thinkers about their finances.

The majority have never spent the time and effort needed to put a solid financial plan in place. The cost from operating with the wrong outlook and not investing $100.00 a month toward your future is huge. Your errors in judgment for those additional *five years* would cost you $254,850 ($100.00 a month compounded at 10% for 40 years equals $637,680, but only $382,830 after 35 years. The difference is $637,680 – 382,830 = $254,850 or opportunity cost). This is money that you cannot get back, because you would have forever given up the chance for time and compounding to work its magic for you.

If you are 40 and have not started your investment plan, I would suggest you get going right away. 15 years of operating the wrong philosophy is long enough. To make matters worse, you have lost out on a cool half million by not understanding how money works. Waiting until 40 to begin saving, means you can only expect a return of $133,790 over the next 25 years of your working life. This might be comforting for some, but I wouldn't get too excited about this anaemic nest egg. For starters we know the value of money erodes over time and what might seem like very reasonable savings based on today's dollar will be small potatoes 20 or 30 years into the future.

Millions of people are quickly running out of time because retirement is no longer far off into the distant future. Age 65 is making a full-out sprint towards them, and they are petrified — or should be — that they will be unprepared for the inevitable collision.

So what can you do if you find yourself short on time with little to no savings for your retirement? Throw up your hands and accept whatever happens? Or is there a card you can still play to help you weather the storm a little better?

Regardless of where you are, there are steps you can take to put you in the driver's seat and control your destiny. They will not be easy, but they will be necessary if you wish to accumulate more than the $133,790 shown above.

We know the key to building wealth is to change small and change often. By changing small I mean taking small, seemingly unimportant steps on a regular basis in order to shape your outlook and design your life. It is the habit of putting aside a part of all you earn regularly and associating with people who have a clear vision and goals for their future. It is developing from the inside out and exercising patience, in order for the natural laws of time and compounding to work their magic. When you change small and change often, you avoid the mistake of trying to get it all in one shot. You build that solid foundation on which you can erect skyscrapers with total confidence.

If you have come to the investment party late in life, you definitely have a tougher time than those who came early and have paced themselves over the years. You won't have what Einstein termed the eighth wonder of the world (time and compounding) on your side. Without this powerful aid you will have to take a very different approach.

At 40 time is no longer your ally when it comes to investing; it is your worst enemy. When time was on your side, a small sum deposited regularly to your bank or investment account could work magic and return a sizable profit. When time is working against you, you lose out on the magic.

So how does your strategy differ when you come late to the party? For starters you will need to invest many more of your hard-earned dollars on a monthly basis to make up for the lost time, and this can be a problem for most people. Secondly, you will need to resist the temptation of putting all your money into the stock market, or you could find yourself in a world of financial trouble if the markets go south on you. Many people got wiped out financially during the recession of 2007-2008, so you would be wise to exercise caution when investing if you wish to preserve your principal.

You cannot predict the markets and could lose your shirt, your lunch, and your home if the market crashes. There are investment vehicles other than the stocks that can provide you a safe return on your money and help you right the ship and sail safely toward your retirement. I will touch on those in a future chapter.

By now it should be easy to see why Warren Buffet, one of the most successful investors of our time, wished he had started his investments much earlier than age 11. He understood the consequences of not having his money in the markets earlier.

Buffet is a wealthy man but his wealth didn't come overnight. His wealth was built on a solid understanding of the rules of money. More importantly, it took decades before the habits he cultivated as a child earned him a sizable fortune. His story is yet another illustration that success comes to those who are willing to follow a few simple habits each and every day.

We need to understand that there are no miracles waiting for us regarding our finance, health, or relationships. Success is the progressive realization of a worthy goal. It doesn't come from winning the lottery. It comes from having a vision, setting goals, and moving toward those goals. You are the director of your life; you design the set, write the script, and play the various roles. It is far better to design a life of your own choosing than to play a role by default.

In closing this chapter, I want to share a story about a couple attending one of my seminars. They clearly did not get the memo about taking full responsibility for their successes and failures.

A few years ago I had the pleasure of being asked to give a Financial Fitness presentation at one of the local libraries in Toronto. It wasn't a very large audience, perhaps 25 people or so, but I vividly recall the events as I led the group through a variety of personal finance topics.

I recall how shocked and amazed I was at the lack of financial literacy among my audience, but in retrospect I realized that my knowledge and understanding wasn't any better than theirs in my early 30s.

Although the presentation was well received, it was quite a sobering message for one gentleman and his wife. They were both in their 40s, but they had not started investing and were nowhere near ready to purchase a home. They knew what they had to do, but had not created a plan to get there. They saw that my discussion focused on the topic of time and compounding and felt it was more geared toward the younger generation who made up the majority of the audience. Since they no longer had the advantage of time and compounding on their side they were stressed.

They clearly missed the whole point of my workshop, which was to get started immediately, regardless of where you are. If you are in your 40's and have not started acquiring assets and putting your financial life in order, you've got to get moving. Time is no longer on your side and this means you will need to contribute significantly more of your income to your investments to make up for the passage of time.

Perspective

Have you ever gone to an amusement park on the final day of the season to catch a ride on your favourite coaster for the last time? I have, and I can recall the huge crowd and the tremendous difficulty I found trying to work my way through the mass of people. Often I couldn't see more than five or ten feet in front of me.

In fact, have you ever been in a situation where the crowd is so thick that you lose sight of what you were looking for in the first place? Pretty soon not only do you stop looking, but you get caught up with the flow of the crowd, leaving your thoughts and wishes behind. In short, we've adjusted to the pace and direction of those around us, and even though we are not sure of the destination, we rationalize that it must be good because everyone else is headed that way.

In reality nothing could be further from the truth. Just because the majority is doing it doesn't make it the right thing to do. The majority of Canadians put aside less than 5% of their yearly earnings for their retirement, but you have to be smarter than that. 5% isn't enough to build a solid financial foundation for you and your family.

Indeed, the real rate of savings is far less flattering than the 5% listed above. A Globe and Mail blog article written by Tavia Grant, on March

1st 2011[8] shows Canada's personal savings rate fell to less than 4.4% for the year 2010. According to BMO Nesbit Burns we are witnessing a flip in historical trends, where Canada's savings rate is much lower than the 5.8% savings rate of Americans[9].

This is one area of your life where you don't want to be average. I remember a comment made by a childhood friend of mine who came from a well-to-do family. Her dad's business was worth more than $5,000,000 at the time and I remember her saying something to the effect that if she was average she would die. My immediate thought was: "How arrogant and pompous!" although I didn't say so out loud.

I now realize that her outlook had been shaped by her surroundings and the upbringing she received. She went to a private school, she lived in an exclusive area of the city, and her dad was a millionaire. For her being average was not part of her daily life, she was being groomed to excel in all she did in order to succeed, and she did just that. Today she is a successful lawyer and mother, and I can tell you she is saving much more than the average Canadian.

There is going to be some self-doubt when you begin to go in the opposite direction from your friends and family members. To be sure, it isn't easy. But easy is no longer an option. If you continue to do what is "easy" (putting nothing toward your future, continue to make errors in judgment), your life will be extremely hard. But if you do what is "hard" (pay yourself first by putting aside a minimum of 10% to start, working on your outlook and setting big goals), your life will be easy.

If you are currently doing what the masses are doing, you need to stop and ask yourself if this is in your future best interest. I say future best interest because, since results come last, the errors in your personal outlook will not show up until years from now. Not disciplining yourself will not hurt you today, and it most likely will not hurt you tomorrow, next month, or even next year. However, the compounded effect of your errors in judgment will in time catch up to you. So embrace the philosophy that easy is not an option and set a course for a better life.

---

8   Grant, Tavia. The Globe and Mail, "Trading Places: U.S. out saves Canada." Last modified 03/01/11. Accessed 11/09/11. http://m.theglobeandmail.com/report-on-business/economy/economy-lab/daily-mix/trading-places-us-outsaves-canada/article1924631/?service=mobile.

9   Cooper, Sherry. BMO Capital Markets-Economic Research, "The Unbearable Lightness of Canadian Interest Rates." Last modified 06/17/11. Accessed 11/02/11. http://www.excellentfuture.ca/sites/default/files/BMO Focus Weekly Digest 17 June 2011.pdf.

I want to take you back to that amusement park for a minute. Picture yourself once again being pushed along with the crowd; walking seems almost effortless (it's easy) as you are being gently nudged in the same direction as the others. You don't know where you are going, but that's all right; you are moving, and you don't have to think about anything.

Contrast that with what it feels like to move against the crowd. What do you see? You're having a much more difficult time of it, aren't you? You come up against obstacles and have to find alternative routes to get around or through those barriers to continue your journey.

Some of those obstacles might be other people, or they might be physical barriers like buildings in your way. When it comes to your financial life, the barriers could be a low-paying job or monthly expenses that seem to consume all you earn. However, you are determined and know exactly where you are going and why it is important for you to get there. Most importantly, you know you must act now or risk staying stuck in the same spot and getting consumed by the crowd. Your goals are kept at the front of your mind, and your persistent approach and determination will not be denied. You know if you do what is hard your life will be easy, but if you give up and fall back into the flow of the crowd your life will be hard.

Eventually, through dogged persistence and determination, you find yourself breaking free from the crowd. Take a deep breath. Doesn't the air feel cleaner? You look around, amazed by the beauty you missed when travelling with the crowd. People are more relaxed and are open to lending a hand to each other, there's no rush and there is plenty of room to manoeuvre without bumping into each other. You can't believe how far you can see into the distance. What an incredible perspective!

Now you have an unobstructed view of the horizon, you can see opportunities that had been surrounding you all that time. Can you see this picture for your life and your finance? Isn't it better than being pushed along without control?

All that you can imagine is within your grasp once you have a fresh new perspective, are committed to your dream, and recognize that easy is not an option. If you are going to succeed financially you will need to brace yourself for the struggles that will inevitably come. One author stated that "Obstacles are the admission price one must pay for success." That's right, the more obstacles you overcome in your life, the greater the probability of your success.

Chapter Three

Taking Control of Your Cash

ousehold debt in Canada reached $1.41 trillion in December 2009, and Statistics Canada reported that the actual debt-to-income ratio reached a record high of 148% in the same year[10]. This means that the average Canadian is spending $1.48 for each dollar earned. You don't have to be a rocket scientist to see the serious trouble millions of Canadians are facing on a daily basis. These are scary numbers, and even though we are in uncertain economic times, millions continue to spend uncontrollably.

A study by Statistics Canada showed that between 1984 and 2009, real average household debt for Canadians more than doubled, from $46,000 to $110,000[11]. Take a look at Chart 1 to see graphically how this addiction to debt has gotten out of control. The main contributor to this increase was mortgage debt. Over this period, the general trend was for average household debt to move in the opposite direction of the interest rate. As interest rates decrease, average household debt increases, because debt becomes more affordable. Beginning in 2002, debt growth accelerated sharply. The financial disaster of 2007/2008 and the threat of a European

---

10 Hurst, Matt. Statistic Canada, "Debt and Family Type in Canada." Last modified 04/21/11. Accessed 10/27/11. http://www.statcan.gc.ca/pub/11-008-x/2011001/article/11430-eng.htm.

11 11 (Hurst 04/21/11)

meltdown in 2012 have done little to curb Canadian's appetite for debt, simply because money is extremely cheap to borrow.

How does this impact you? Well, let's put some actual numbers into this scenario to help you understand how our Canadian addiction to debt is destroying the hope of millions of people ever achieving financial fitness.

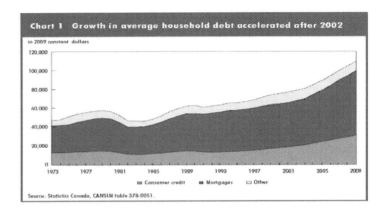

If we were to take the national debt and divide it evenly among all Canadians regardless of age, each of us would be responsible for approximately $42,000. With this burden on our shoulders, it is easy to see why millions in our society will end up broke and embarrassed at the age of 65. Take a look at Chart 2.

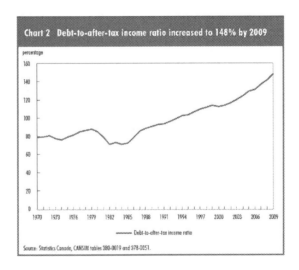

We know that total household income is the key to understanding debt. Data taken from national accounts, show that on average between 1970 and 2009 disposable income per household grew by 37% after adjusting for inflation. This increase in income enabled more households to take on additional debt, and they did.

One would think that as income goes up we would be able to reduce our debts, but it is quite the opposite. Despite growth in disposable income, the debt-to-income ratio climbed continually between 1984 and 2009, as increases in household debt outpaced growth in income.

By 1994, debt levels were greater than incomes, meaning households owed more than they earned. For example, in 1990, total personal and unincorporated business debt was equivalent to 93% of after-tax income. By 2009, total debt was equivalent to 148% of income (see Chart 2).

Many people have accepted this increased debt load as the new normal for a consumer-oriented society. But the problem with this kind of thinking is if interest rates were to rise by three percentage points, the debt-to-income ratio would have to fall between 125% and 130% for interest payments on the debt to remain the same. The truth is that many people will be hurt once rates go up, simply because they will not be able to meet the higher payments. We can't remain ignorant and believe that the low-interest environment Canadians are now enjoying will last forever.

When I was young I often heard that "it is best to learn from our own mistakes." Although there is value in this statement, I believe it is far wiser to learn from the mistakes of others. If we look at history we can often see the mistakes and successes of those who have gone before us. We have only to decide on the results we want to create and which path will take us there.

We can look at our neighbours to the south and learn from their mistakes in order to chart a different course. Unless Canadians do a quick about-face and rein in their spending, there will be "blood in the streets" much like what we have witnessed with the United States.

The Causes of Debt

So what is the root cause of the poor money habits we have as a society? Is it greed, envy, or ignorance? Some blame it on ignorance and collectively point their fingers at the government and our educational system for having failed its citizens.

I must admit there was a time in my life when I would have agreed our poor financial knowledge is a direct result of our schools and governments' failure to prepare us for the real world. However, I have matured and realize that the first step to lasting change is to stop blaming others and take full responsibility for my actions and the results I create.

Successful people do not make excuses. They have given up the blame game and take 100% responsibility for the things that happen in their lives. When you decide to embrace this perspective, your life will begin to change in dramatic ways.

Don't get me wrong, our schools need to do a much better job of preparing our students for the real world. But we must be very careful not to point fingers and put all the responsibility on the shoulders of others. Those who are not willing to change are often looking for someone else to take the blame. Don't let that be you; if you have messed up like I did, take full responsibility and commit to doing things right from now on. *Always remember that when you point your finger at someone else, there are three fingers pointing back at you.*

So our schools messed up and our governments messed up — now what? Well, for starters we have to become more financially literate. No one is going to come to rescue you. My financial life started to change when I made the decision that it would have to be up to me. Your financial picture will change as well, but only if you decide to take the road less travelled.

The current uncertainty in the markets about the European debt crisis, along with increased household debt, has many people and even governments talking about the need for a financial literacy curriculum in our schools. All I can say is it's about time!

It's sad that a skill so basic, yet so vital to successfully navigating the world of finance has been neglected by governments all around the world until now. Why now? Could it be that our governments have finally come to the realization that they cannot be all things to all people and that by creating a society dependent on the Canada Pension Plan (CPP) and Old Age Security (OAS) they have in the process created millions of citizens' content with living mediocre lives without a true passion and purpose?

Yes, *financial literacy* is needed, and a call for a revamped curriculum is a good start for future generations. However, that will do little to protect those who are already hurting financially.

Times are changing, and governments around the globe are starting to make deficit reduction their number one priority. Never before in the history of the world have so many economies been so closely tied to each other. This has created cause for concern, because if one country catches a cold it is now much easier to spread those symptoms around the world.

The European debt crisis is a great example of our changing economies and the risk of global contagion. If the EU countries are not able to rein in their deficits, create jobs and expand their economies, the impact on countries around the world could be catastrophic.

Our federal Finance Minister weighed in on the EU's inability to get its house in order amid growing concerns that Canada is also exposed to European credit crisis. In November 2011, Jim Flaherty issued stern warnings to Europe in a speech to the Canadian Club[12]. He likened the behaviour of some European countries to a person repeatedly maxing out credit cards:

> *Households don't operate like this and neither should countries. When your credit card is maxed out, you don't go out and get another one and continue to accumulate interest at 18 per cent. Instead, you figure out a way to restrain your spending and you increase your payments to reduce your debt.*

Flaherty was asked about Canada's exposure and the potential risk should Europe fail to make the corrections needed to shore up its economy. He said that, although Canada has a very sound financial system we would not be immune. "The danger is if we have a global crisis. That would affect credit markets everywhere."

The Minister has been very open in his criticism of Europe's inability to deal with this crisis and used a beautiful household analogy as a way of explaining how Europe got into this mess in the first place:

> *You make difficult choices to put your family's finances on a structurally stronger footing by re-evaluating how much you spend and where. Otherwise, you lose control of your destiny, either to a credit counsellor who will unilaterally impose harsh remedial measures or, worse yet, to bankruptcy court.*

This is a simplification of what is going on in Europe, but it presents a perfect analogy on the importance of having a sound financial plan to

---

12   Kilpatric, Sean. Canada Press, "Flaherty calls Europe's debt woes 'dire'." Last modified 11/25/2011. Accessed 12/15/11. http://www.cbc.ca/news/business/story/2011/11/25/flaherty-economy-speech.html.

protect our families and the need to re-evaluate our finances from time to time in order to keep us on track to achieve our goals.

Canadians need to wake up and start paying closer attention to what is happening in the economy. We can't continue our insatiable appetite for debt and remain ignorant to the inevitable disasters to come. We need to start saving more, or risk living way below our means at a time in our lives when we should be enjoying the fruits of our labour. The November 2011 Ontario throne speech warned of major budget cuts to come. Ottawa is cutting thousands of jobs in the public service and freezing government wages. The fact that this is occurring at precisely the wrong time is irrelevant. Hard times are already upon us.

The financial crisis of 2007/2008 has put our government on high alert — and baby boomers in a funk, because many of them lived their lives without a plan. For many people this is the first time in their lives that they have actually started thinking about tomorrow instead of focusing only on today. This is yet one more reason we are seeing increased media attention on financial literacy.

Reining in your spending

Today companies use the media to compete against each other, paying major dollars to increase market share. Does it work? Of course! For many successful companies, the money spent on advertising is a drop in the bucket compared to the increased revenues generated by increased brand loyalty. Companies strategically market their products to the "got to have it now" segment of the population, as they know this group often shops on impulse and wants to be the first to have the latest toy.

The "got to have it now" generation is largely responsible for the historic increase we have seen in consumer spending over the past 20 years. The internet has effectively eliminated the cooling-off period that used to exist for many shoppers. In fact, the revenues generated from internet sales in Canada continue to hit record highs, and we can only expect those numbers to swell as the economy picks up. A Statistics Canada survey entitled E-Commerce: Shopping on the internet[13] concluded that Canadians used the Internet in 2009 to place orders for goods and services valued at $15.1 billion, up from $12.8 billion in 2007.

13   McKeown, Larry, and Ben Veenhof. Stats Canada, "E-commerce: Shopping on the Internet." Last modified 10/27/10. Accessed 11/23/11. http://www.statcan.gc.ca/daily-quotidien/100927/dq100927a-eng.htm.

From 2004 to 2009 Canadian internet purchases have increased from $3 billion to $15.1 billion, a more than fivefold increase. These numbers can only be expected to increase dramatically in the coming years as more and more people get connected to the internet and start using their smart phones to shop online. So how do we correct it? Good question: let's begin.

Assets and Liabilities

In the previous chapter we spoke about the habit of saving being the fundamental principle that must be established if you are to build a successful financial future. Once you have made the habit automatic, you need to apply step number two in the process to wealth: to eliminate or control unnecessary spending.

I am not saying we should hoard our money and never buy the occasional thing that catches our fancy. To hoard money is a sin and it does you no good to hold on to it and fear spending it. Remember that you can't take it with you. So we do need to enjoy some of the things money can buy, and those might even be things on your wish or want list and not only your necessities list. However, you have to exercise caution and not jeopardize your future financial fitness.

Before we get too far into this chapter, I want to point out the difference between what is considered an asset and what is a liability. Once you have an understanding of the concept, you will be able to make the right decisions about how you spend your money. Those who have achieved financial independence definitely know the difference. In fact I would go so far as to say that without a clear understanding of the difference between assets and liabilities you cannot create a successful financial fitness blueprint.

Simply — an asset is something that puts money into your pocket and a liability is something that takes money out of your pocket.

Now this statement by itself may still not give you a clear understanding; but by the end of this book your increased financial literacy will allow you to make the right decisions about your money to grow your wealth.

Let's take a good look at how Canadians are spending, and decide if they are purchasing assets or liabilities. When I was in my early 20s I was just like the average consumer. I purchased many of the new gadgets believing the hype about how they would change my life.

But for me, and I would suspect many of you, the lustre quickly wore off these purchases. They didn't live up to my expectations, and besides, my friends were telling me about how their version of the same product was better than the one I bought. Many of the items we felt we could never do without, that were purchased on impulse, became collector's items under our beds or locked away in the corner of our closets.

Today I weigh the cost before every purchase, and I would suggest you do the same. When you spend a few minutes weighing the cost to your financial future you will start making better decisions with your money. You need to ask yourself before each purchase: Is this going to increase or decrease my wealth? Or, more simply: Is this putting money into my pocket or taking it away? If you are comfortable knowing that the purchase is going to take money out of your pocket and not generate increased value for you, you might still make the purchase; but at least you will have given it some thought and won't have purchased on impulse.

Of course, it would be a practical impossibility to make only purchases that bring you an increased return on your money on a daily basis. However, the important point here is to limit the purchases that take money away from you (liabilities) in favour of those that add value to your bottom line (assets).

I want you to take a moment to write your response about whether each of the following items would be considered an asset or a liability. Don't skip this part, it is important to take stock and find out exactly where you are with your understanding of how money works.

Asset or Liability

1. Buying the newest-model flat-screen television because it is on sale
2. Upgrading to a new car to get better gas mileage
3. Spending $200.00 to attend a weekend seminar listening to professional speakers on the importance of setting goals
4. Going out for lunch with co-workers three or four times a week
5. Buying books and audio on personal development and financial fitness
6. Borrowing money from your credit card to purchase RRSPs
7. Purchasing a home and renting out two of the rooms
8. Paying a coach to help you learn the ins and outs of real estate investing
9. Donating to charities on a regular and consistent basis

How did you do? Do you think you got them all correct? Let us take a look. If you said buying that flat-screen television was an asset because you got it on sale and saved $300.00 wrong.

Buying depreciating items on sale does not make them an asset. A television cannot increase your wealth. In fact, I would say it is probably one of the greatest wealth robbers of all time. Think of how much of your valuable time is spent watching drivel that has absolutely no intrinsic value for you. How many courses could you have completed with the time wasted on television, or how many books could you have read? Question number one is clearly a liability. Turn off your television and turn on your creative mind to the limitless possibilities available to you.

Buying a new car to save a few dollars on fuel is definitely a liability. Yes, fuel economy is important, but to spend $15,000 to $20,000 on a new car just to save a few dollars on gas is a colossal waste of your money. Your car depreciates by as much as 10% to 20% in value the minute you drive it off the lot. If you bought a $20,000 car it would be worth as little as $16,000 after you left the dealership. Ask yourself: Will you be saving $4,000 in gas because of this purchase? I don't believe you will.

Spending $200.00 to attend a weekend course on goal setting is money well spent, and should be considered an asset. A word of caution about attending seminars: There are many wonderful speakers and teachers out there with terrific messages that can awaken the spirit and ignite the fire that once burned brightly in us. However, be careful that you do not become a "seminar junkie," going from one seminar to the next, weekend after weekend. Know exactly what you want to learn and pursue it with tenacity, but above all apply the teachings.

Going out with your co-workers three or four times a week might seem like a good idea because you get to bond, but the cost to your future wealth is enormous. Just imagine, even at the modest cost of $25.00 per week for lunch, how much money you are blowing in the wind. There are 52 weeks in the year, and let's say for argument's sake you go out with your co-workers a total of 40 weeks. You have blown a cool $1,000 to discuss office politics and listen to each other complain. Wouldn't it be nicer to get a $1,000 bonus at the end of the year? Well, you can give yourself that bonus by eliminating this cost.

Purchasing books and audio recordings of material that will help you elevate your understanding of successful life principles is definitely an asset. It was Zig Ziglar who coined the term "automobile university." Since the majority of adults spend several hours travelling to and from work on a regular basis, why not purchase some educational CDs and increase your knowledge while driving? This one strategy has been invaluable to me and has resulted in the increased knowledge I have acquired about real estate investing and success in general. As you might guess, this is easy to do, but also easy not to do. The thing is, you won't see changes immediately after listening to these CDs, but the gradual and compound effect over time will help to change your outlook and ultimately your life. Do yourself a favour and make the investment into your own brighter future. If you are a subway rider, get some eBooks and read on your iPad.

Borrowing money from a high-interest credit card to purchase RRSPs without a guaranteed return is a definite liability. If you are going to borrow money for an investment, your return on the investment must be greater than the cost of borrowing the funds. Don't get led down this road. Pay off your credit card debts before you put money into your RRSP, because the interest to service those debts is probably much higher than what you could hope to expect from the returns on the investment.

Buying a home and renting out a room or two is definitely an asset, especially if you can carry the mortgage on your income. Many people purchase homes and never think about making that purchase a profitable investment. When I had my second home, I had two rooms that sat vacant for seven out of eight years. I finally saw my error, but it took seven years of lost income before I got it. Buying a home and renting out the rooms is a definite asset.

Paying a coach to help accelerate you toward your goals is a definite asset. If someone can help you shave years off the time needed to achieve your financial goals, then you need to seek out the coaching necessary to do so. Make sure the person comes with a proven track record and is still in the game doing the things you are striving to do. I am 100% behind coaching and mentorship, because a good coach or mentor can help you identify what is impeding your progress.

Donating to a charity regularly is definitely an asset. For those who think they are too poor to give to others, perish the thought. If you continue in that frame of mind, you will have a very difficult time escaping the clutches of poverty. It is said, "Where your attention goes your energy flows." Do not see yourself as anything but financially fit even when the chips are down. When you really break it down, it is the giving to others that opens up the floodgates for you to receive. Now if you are really strapped and can't afford regular monetary contributions to a charity or cause, you can volunteer your time. In many cases your time is more valuable and goes further than a $50 bill.

Now that you know the difference between an asset and a liability, you are in a better position to make good purchasing decisions with your money.

How do you spend your money?

Some people will swear that budgets work and others will tell you they are a waste of time. As for myself, I cannot say that I ever used one with any regularity when I was younger. However, there were times when that might not have been such a bad idea.

Many feel that budgeting puts too many restrictions on them and that they should be able to spend their money any way they want. On this point I would have to agree with them. It is, after all, their money, and if they want to blow it all without thinking of how this impacts their future wealth, that is their right.

However, if you are paying attention you understand that unless we take a close look at our spending habits we will not be able to see the cash leaks that need our attention. Fortunately for me, one of my mentors turned me around on the importance of budgeting for success.

Today I use a budget tracker to get a clear picture of how I am spending. My strategy is to take a snapshot of my spending over a one-month period. I must admit that this requires considerable discipline, but you can begin by tracking only a few weeks the first time you get started. I go through this process twice a year, because it allows me to take stock of my spending habits and make timely corrections.

Once you have written down all your monthly financial obligations (including expenses for entertainment) you will have a clearer picture of how much money you truly have to work with (discretionary income). I would then suggest you keep a careful record of every purchase made during that month and write these down in a journal or notebook.

At the end of the month (or the second week if you are just starting out), give yourself a few hours to sit down and go over the list of items you have purchased. You might be shocked to see where much of your money is going. Have you developed some bad habits? Do you find yourself at the local Tim Hortons or Starbucks several times a week dropping money on specialty coffees? Remember there is a cost to every decision you make about your money. Are you weighing the cost?

Let me just clarify once more. You cannot take your money to the grave, so I am not suggesting you boycott Tim Hortons or Starbucks. However, if you are strapped for cash, I mean really having some financial challenges; you might want to take a hard look at such things. Do you really need the unlimited cable package, or could you get along with basic or no cable? Do you need that iPad, or the laptop and desktop computers to surf the internet, or are these purchases simply to keep up with the latest gadgets so you can have conversations with your friends about your new toys? Do you need the iPhone with the most expensive data plan or can you get by without it?

I can't answer these questions for you, but far too many are living life like they have it all in order to impress their friends, while their financial fitness blueprint remains tattered and torn. The next time you make a purchase decision to impress someone, remember this fact: most people spend the majority of their time thinking about themselves and their own situations; they have little time to be concerned about you. Bottom line: the people you are trying to impress don't care what you have or don't have. It's all your perception.

Budgeting for Success

One of the keys to ensuring your financial fitness is to take full responsibility for your life. One way of taking full responsibility is to put together a solid plan for how you will spend your money. Without a plan you will end up moving through life like a ship without a rudder, wallowing around hoping one day you will reach dry land.

But how does one go about putting a proper budget together? Is there a proven formula that works? The truth is, there are many formulas that work, but each will depend on the goal you have in mind. When you have clear goals for what you want to achieve in your financial life, the steps for creating a proper budget that you can stick with become rather easy.

If you are serious about becoming financially fit, then the **60, 15, 5, 20 Formula** is what I would recommend. Here is how I break this down:

The 60, 15, 5, 20 Formula

- *Sixty percent* of your monthly income will be put aside to meet your daily expenses, what we call life's necessities. These expenses will include items like your mortgage or rent, food, home insurance, clothing, etc. Now, for some of you, this will prove very difficult, especially if you have children and a new mortgage. However, if you have not purchased above your means and are disciplined enough, you would be surprised at exactly how creative you can become when it comes to finding extra money.

- *Fifteen percent* of your paycheque will be used to satisfy your wants and desires. We have a lot of those, don't we? Unfortunately, neither you nor I have the time or the resources necessary to satisfy all our wants, so we have to decide what is important to us when it comes to allocating this 15%. Maybe you love travelling and can't resist that sell-off vacation to your tropical paradise. Go for it! You deserve a break. Don't stress about making this purchase, as you've earned the right to enjoy some of the fruits of your labour. Maybe you like entertaining friends and family, so the idea of a brand-new entertainment unit and monthly gatherings is what gets you excited. Go for it! Just make sure you don't exceed the allotted 15%.

- *The remaining 25%* is your seed money: 5% will go to charity and 20% will be used to build your financial house. Does putting 20% of your income towards future wealth creation seem impossible from where you sit? I can already hear you saying yes, but here is a question for you: If others have done it, isn't it possible that you can do the same?

Twenty percent is significantly higher than the 10% minimum normally recommended, but there is a reason for this. Paying yourself first with 10% of all you earn will provide you with a good retirement and I believe everyone can do this regardless of income. Paying yourself 20% a year over your working life will provide you with enough income to live the life you've always wanted. You have choices; it all depends on what you have envisioned for your life.

Paying yourself 20% is not easy, but I hope you have come to understand easy is not an option when it comes to securing your financial future. If you are willing to commit to this kind of saving, you will see dramatic improvements in your financial fortunes in five to ten years — and just imagine what 25 to 30 years of such savings would mean for you and your family!

I will go further into why I recommend the 60, 15, 5, 20 formula for financial success in a later chapter. For now we will shift gears in order to discuss one of the cardinal errors in judgment that prevents millions of people from ever achieving financial stability, let alone financial freedom.

Delayed Gratification

We must all suffer from one of two pains: the pain of discipline or the pain of regret. The difference is discipline weighs ounces while regret weighs tons.

—Jim Rohn

Those who follow a disciplined approach to saving and spending are much more likely to achieve financial fitness than those who are undisciplined. It is often difficult for us to see the errors in our outlook unless we have a clear plan for what it is we want to accomplish. A plan allows us to develop the discipline needed to guide us to accomplishing our goals.

Another way of looking at it is *discipline is the bridge between goals and success.* When you apply discipline and have a clear plan for your future, it is easy to make corrections and stay on course because you can clearly see when you are going off course. Those striving to achieve financial freedom can usually put their wants on hold and delay gratification for a later time. They see the bigger picture, because they have clearly defined goals and are not willing to sabotage their own progress.

On the flip side, the "name it and claim it" person sees what he wants and will go to any length to get it regardless of the cost to the bottom line. He sees the parts of the picture (immediate gratification) as more valuable than the whole (the "big picture"). But the misplaced value he gives to immediate gratification prevents him from ever developing a solid plan for something bigger. His day-to-day existence and lack of discipline leads to an unfulfilled life of regret and underachievement.

This group can be classified as "chasers" — they chase every new fad, and covet what others have in order to appear that they are on top of the world. They will put themselves in debt, move to the bigger house in the upscale community, all to keep up appearances or impress neighbours and friends.

They want to "keep up with the Joneses." The trouble is they are so self-centered that they seldom take the time to study the Joneses or have a conversation around the Joneses' personal philosophy on money. If they did, they might realize that their neighbours are avid readers, committed to lifelong learning in order to improve their financial fitness.

In fact the Joneses have worked hard on getting themselves to the point where they command a greater income because of the increased value they bring to the marketplace. Our chasers or "name it and claim it" group see none of the changes that have taken place with the Joneses. They have never taken the time to look at the bigger picture and devise a solid game plan of how to create their lives by design. They are misguided and have not worked on correcting the errors in their own outlook. They operate from envy and jealousy and believe that if others have it, so should they.

This lack of discipline and understanding about financial literacy has crippled millions. By the time they realize what the Joneses have been doing on the inside to attract the things on the outside it is far too late. The pain of regret is so heavy that the financial burden on their shoulder cannot be shrugged off. If you are going to succeed financially you must master delayed gratification and stay focused on the goals you have set for yourself.

Where Does the Money Go?

Let's address the issue. We have all heard that there is good debt and bad debt. So how can one tell the difference?

A good debt allows you to build up your assets (put money in your pocket) and a bad debt takes money out of your pocket (liabilities). It is important to understand this point. Some people have outstanding debts totaling millions of dollars to the banks, but because they are mortgages on properties they are considered assets not liabilities. These individuals know how to successfully leverage the banks' money to grow their wealth, and the bank cooperates as long as the mortgages can be covered by the rents from the properties.

On the other hand we have individuals who owe hundreds of thousands for the purchase of consumer items like cars, boats, home furnishings, and stuff. These individuals have purchased liabilities. These purchases, unlike real estate, will not appreciate in value and cannot generate income for the owner. In fact, those who spend the bulk of their money acquiring liabilities are only a heartbeat from financial ruin.

Lack of financial literacy is at the heart of many people's decision to buy their wants on credit. Many don't understand the danger of credit card use or even know the difference between fixed and revolving credit. This lack of understanding about how money works is largely responsible for the increased debt many Canadians have on their shoulders.

Tips to Reduce Your Expenses

Sometimes all we need is a little more information to expand our awareness and get us on the right track. This is why I continue to attend seminars and read books regularly. If you decide to read for 30 to 60 minutes every day, not only will your knowledge and awareness improve, but you will be in a better position to make informed decisions. There are simple things you can do to reduce some of your monthly expenses, and all that is required is for you to sit down and unleash your creative mind. I have listed a few ideas below to get you started.

Banking

Not all banks are created equal. Some, like ING, ICICI, and HSBC, will do their best to lure you away from the big banks like Scotia, TD, and RBC. These smaller banks have done a nice job of providing clients with higher-interest savings accounts and no-fee banking. If you have money that you are holding in a savings account you might want to consider switching to one of the above-mentioned banks.

Another thought worth considering is calling your lender and asking them to reduce the interest rate you are currently paying on your charge cards. Make sure you ask for someone in a position to make decisions about rate cuts; the person answering the phone is not your first option. This one simple request can add significant dollars to your bottom line by reducing your borrowing cost.

Own Your Own Business

I can see the look of disbelief on your face. But I am being totally serious when I tell you to own your own business. I am not telling you to go out and buy a Tim Hortons franchise or anything like that (but if you have the cash such a franchise wouldn't be a bad idea). Owning your business does not have to be costly. You can find a home-based business that will cost you less than a few hundred dollars to get going. That small investment could save you thousands in taxes, but most importantly, it could provide another source of income to move you closer to financial fitness. Visit Yahoo Site Builder to download their template and build your website, or do some research on direct marketing companies or multi-level marketing (MLM) companies in your area.

Cool Savings

Reduce your home heating bill by installing a programmable electronic thermostat. This might sound like a commonsense thing to do, but many people who have an electronic thermostat never take the time to set them so the temperatures are lower when they are away from the house and during sleeping hours. This one simple tip can save you hundreds of dollars. Visit Energy shop (www.energyshop.com) for tips on saving energy in your home.

Yours to Discover

I often wonder how those with large families afford to take annual vacations without breaking the bank.

If you have a family, then you know how expensive trips and outings can be. Where can we go, and how much can we afford to spend are topics that can often consume hours of your precious time. You want to give your family a vacation because you believe all work and no play makes for a dull upbringing for your kids. But how do you enjoy those priceless moments with your family year after year without breaking the bank?

A terrific site is Attractions Ontario (www.attractionsontario.ca). Not only do you get some great discounts and savings on your family outings, but you get the added bonus of exploring and experiencing the beauty of Ontario.

Embrace Technology

Got junk? Sell it on eBay or Kijiji. You won't believe the things people will pay money to have in their homes. If you have some items that are just taking up space in your home and can't imagine for a minute ever using them again, sell them. You've often heard that one man's junk is another man's treasure, so get rid of your junk and make someone else the beneficiary of your stuff. The great thing about this is that you might end up making some good dollars for your efforts. So take a day and get going. If nothing else, at least you will have more room in your home.

The Skinny on Debt
Fixed Credit

Fixed, or closed-end, loans are negotiated between the individual and the lender. You agree on the exact amount you will borrow, how much you will pay back monthly, amount of time needed to do so, and the rate of interest. Examples are school loans owed to the government, car loans, mortgages, and loans from the bank to fund your RRSP contribution.

Revolving Credit

Unlike your fixed debt, revolving debt has no fixed monthly payments, offers several payment options, and requires a monthly minimum payment. An example would be your home equity line or a credit card. The most important terms to understand are the amount owed and the interest rate being charged, as this will have the most impact on your bottom line. Far too many people take this for granted and end up in debt way beyond their means.

It is said that the average person carries up to five credit cards, and I guess that would make me average, seeing as how I have access to money from five different lenders. Notice that I said I have access to money from five lenders, not that I carry five credit cards. If you are actually carrying five credit cards on your person, I would strongly encourage you to change that and keep your cards at home. One or two should more than do the job, regardless of your spending habits.

If you don't have five credit cards, don't run out and get any more, because you don't need them. To be totally honest, I think three cards is the ideal number, and just because the average person carries five doesn't make it something to strive for. Remember, the average person lacks the financial literacy to use credit to their advantage and gets taken for a ride by our financial institutions.

You must do all you can to start thinking and moving with those that are above average when it comes to their understanding of personal finance. Keep in mind that our banking systems love Mr. and Mrs. Joe Average. Their bottom lines are bolstered every year by the insatiable wants of Mr. and Mrs. Joe Average. Their lack of financial understanding is a cash cow for the banks.

In the book *Debt Cures*, Kevin Trudeau reveals that the banks earn more than 50% of their profits from fees charged to you — the consumer.

Late fees, fees charged for insufficient funds, activation fees, annual premium card fees, processing fees, administration fees, and on and on. In 2005 credit card companies in the United States spent $5 billion on advertising and made more than $30 billion in profits[14]. How much of that did you receive? You can avoid some of these costly expenses, but you must become a serious student of the money game.

Fixed Versus Revolving Credit

The following examples will show the high cost of one type of credit versus the other. It is the lack of understanding of the differences between these two types of credit that gets the majority of people into financial trouble. Once you educate yourself about the differences, you will be on your way to taking control of your financial destiny.

For simplicity we will use whole numbers so our math is easy to follow. For our examples below we are going to use $5,000 as the loan amount for both the fixed and the revolving credit line.

Example 1: Fixed Credit Line

You are desperate for a loan to tie you over because you have run into a financial roadblock. Unfortunately, you don't have any money; but your friend knows someone who apparently knows someone willing to give you a loan at a price. You are desperate, your credit is shot and you have no hope of getting a loan from the bank. So reluctantly you follow your friend to meet Louie the Butcher. Louie takes a liking to you and offers you a fixed loan at 18% return on his money. You are torn, but you accept the deal.

Louie is a savvy investor and has read *The Financial Fitness Blueprint* a few times over. He lends you $5,000, but sets the terms right there for you so there is no misunderstanding about what your responsibility will be each and every month. Louie goes on to explain how the interest is calculated and exactly how long it will take you to pay off your debt. He also takes the time to show you how much the entire loan plus interest will cost for the term of the loan. Here is the breakdown; $5,000 at 18% interest, paying $150.00 a month will take three years and 11 months to be paid in full. The total interest on the debt will be $1,984. You feel better knowing this in advance, and are confident you will be able to pay back

---

14   Trudeau, Kevin. Debt Cures, Phoenix, AZ: Equity Press, 2008.

the loan and the interest in the time frame outlined. You and Louie shake hands to seal the deal.

Example 2: Revolving Credit Line

It is your turn to host the Super Bowl party. You find yourself in the impossible position of needing $5,000, because you have to have that flat-screen television with surround sound. You don't want to let your friends down by showing the game on your old 32-inch colour TV. Only the 56-inch flat-screen will do the trick. You don't have the $5,000 saved for this purchase — in fact; you have been living paycheque to paycheque and off your credit card for months. If not for the leftovers your mom sends over, you would be in even worse financial shape.

You decide to throw caution to the wind and buy the TV. Wait until the guys see this, you beam as you leave the store. Unlike Louie the Butcher, the sales person at Best Buy didn't read *The Financial Fitness Blueprint.* She gave you no advice on the true cost of this purchase or how long it would take you to pay off your debt. Frankly she doesn't really care if you can afford to pay your bill or not, she's just glad she is able to close the sale.

Here is what she didn't tell you — but you really can't blame her because it is very unlikely that she knows this in the first place. The $5,000 purchase you made on your credit card is a revolving debt. This means you can still go out and make additional purchases, pay them down and make more purchases. You can also make additional purchases on top of the entertainment system that will simply be added to your earlier debt if you choose. In short, there is no fixed time period being imposed for you to pay off the TV. You have some flexibility in how you pay the credit card company. You can pay the 3% minimum or $10, whichever is greater, for the life of the loan.

You should know that paying the minimum amount is not in your best interest, as it will end up taking 18 years and 10 months to pay off the loan while costing you $4,801 in interest. Surprised?

Credit Card Blues

Is there any good news when it comes to taking on credit? Of course, but let's first take a look at the negative side of credit. If you are not well disciplined, there is a temptation to use your charge card to make unnecessary impulse purchases. The payment terms are too flexible, and many people, because they lack financial intelligence, wait too long to pay their bills and get hammered with late fee payments sometimes greater than the amount that is actually owed on their card. Terms and conditions of the loan are not fixed, and the bank has the right to change the terms without notice when they want to (read the fine print). Missing your minimum payment can often increase your interest rate, putting you more and more in debt.

Some people get in trouble financially, not because they can't afford to pay their bills, but because they have developed poor habits along the way. How many of you get your bills and pay them as soon as humanly possible? I make it a habit not to leave a bill unpaid for more than three days. I also open every piece of mail I get and put the bills right on my laptop, as a reminder each and every day to get it taken care of. The reason I use my laptop, of course, is that I am always on my computer writing or looking at real estate. This habit ensures that I never miss a payment and keeps my credit score in good standing.

If you take on a debt, you have to be disciplined enough to pay it off promptly. Don't put off paying your bills from month to month. It's your debt, so take full responsibility for it. Remember, successful people don't make excuses. Don't mess with your credit by avoiding your debts. Warren Buffet said, "Habits are too light to be felt until they are too heavy to be broken." When you develop poor habits with your money it ends up costing you in the future. Your creditworthiness is questioned by lenders who have access to your credit history and credit report. Your character and integrity will come into question and you will not be trusted with more.

Those who carefully oversee their spending habits are always trusted with more, and that is why they continue to increase their wealth. Their understanding and application of the principles that govern how money works, allow them to take advantage of all the opportunities available. Those same opportunities are available to all of us. But only those who are disciplined and have practised the simple things so often taken for granted by 95% of the population ever truly capitalize on them.

Good News about Credit Cards

The good thing for you who understand credit is that you have money available when you need it. You might find yourself in the enviable position of being able to borrow money at a lower interest rate. I was once offered credit from one company of $15,000 for nine months at an interest rate of 0.9%, and you better believe I found a way to leverage that money to make more!

Credit cards offer flexible payment options (and that can be seen as a positive), but I would advise you to pay your bills in full when they are due to avoid paying interest. I understand some things just can't be paid off in one shot, because life does throw the occasional curve ball. However, if you ever find you have bitten off more than you can chew, you might want to consider the following option. Switch your debt to a low-interest card, or to your lines of credit, which are usually at a lower interest. Your goal is to pay as little in interest as possible on all your debts.

Another positive to credit cards is unlike a personal loan, which has to be used for a specific purchase, you can use your credit card to purchase anything you want, and this is a very attractive feature for most people. The convenience of carrying plastic instead of cash is also seen as a positive, though it takes discipline to keep the card in your wallet and not spend money on a whim.

Leveraging debt

Using credit to purchase assets that appreciate is an example of leverage. If the purchase results in more money going into your pocket after paying back the loan with interest, you have used leverage in your favour.

The purchase of a car using your line of credit is not a good example of leverage, as the car depreciates immediately after you drive away. However, purchasing an investment property is a good example of positive leverage if the purchase puts money into your pocket after the interest for the loan is paid.

Robert Kiyosaki, author of *Increasing your Financial IQ* and *Rich Dad, Poor Dad*, provides some great reasons for why real estate is such a powerful vehicle for wealth creation. I would encourage you to pick up one of these books. If you already have them in your library, I would suggest you read them again and start applying the principles. I began my real estate investing after reading *Rich Dad, Poor Dad*, and I found the ideas invaluable.

It is very important for each of us to know where we stand when it comes to our creditworthiness. If you have been paying your bills on time and are not way over your head in debt, chances are your credit score is good. However, as with everything in life, errors do occur from time to time.

Therefore, it is important for everyone, regardless of the level of their financial literacy, to get a copy of their credit report. There might be errors that if left uncorrected, might have negative repercussions on your credit score.

I would suggest you get a copy of your credit report at least twice a year and go over them carefully. As an investor I make it a priority to know my score, treat it like gold, and protect it at all costs, and you should do the same.

To get a copy of your report and score, contact Equifax or Trans Union, the two main consumer credit reporting agencies. Your credit score can be ordered online for less than $30.00.

This document will reveal the level of your perceived creditworthiness. A score above 650 points is considered good; at that level most lending institutions will work with you. If your score is 750 or more, you are managing your credit very well, and should have no problem qualifying for bank loans, home mortgages, etc.

It is worth knowing your score before you decide on any major purchases. A great guide and resource that will provide you with invaluable information about credit and eliminating debt is the book *Debt Cures* by Kevin Trudeau, which is definitely worth buying or picking up from your local library.

Reduce Your Debt Ratio

As mentioned earlier, I believe having three credit cards is ideal for the majority of us. Consider the following example. Many of us have often heard that if you are in financial trouble you should cut up all your credit cards except one. I don't agree. I believe it is too simplistic, and has a potential cost in the long run.

For some people credit is like an accident waiting to happen. They are compulsive shoppers and regardless of how far in debt they are, they continue to spend with reckless abandon. For them it would be good advice to give up their credit cards altogether and put their financial lives in order. But for you and me, having a few credit cards is actually a good thing.

Here's why. If you have only one credit card, with a limit of $15,000, and you need to make a big purchase (possibly an emergency home repair or, worse, to bury a family member), you have no option but to put the entire purchase on the card. This will negatively affect your credit rating, because of the high debt load you would be carrying. But if you have three cards, you can split the cost of the items across them. This reduces your debt load per card to a manageable 33% and has the added benefit of building your credit history because you do business with more than one lender. Whenever possible, don't keep a balance on your credit cards that is greater than 30% of the limit you've been given.

Whatever you do, avoid paying only the minimum on your cards. It does you no good and only fattens the pockets of your bankers. Try your best not to carry a balance on your credit from month to month. If you can't avoid this, you might consider taking the following steps to reduce your expenses and keep more money in your pocket.

Call your credit card companies and ask them to lower your interest rate. You will be surprised at how many will do that for you simply because you asked! Believe me, it works — I have used it more than once.

Secondly, call the companies and find out if they have a promotion. Most have regular promotions throughout the year. If they have a promotion (sometimes as low as 2.99%) for six months, tell them you would like to make a balance transfer to their credit card. This will allow you to move your balance from a high-interest to a low-interest card. The beauty of this strategy is that your credit score is not affected, because you are not applying for additional credit. If you have only one credit card, you are not going to be able to utilize this strategy.

For those contemplating getting a mortgage, make sure you use a mortgage broker and don't shop from bank to bank. If you have a good relationship with a particular mortgage specialist at your local branch and you know he or she will give you a good deal, by all means go for it. But even if you don't have such a relationship, a mortgage broker will usually work to get you the best interest rates and terms available.

Notice I said a broker will *usually* work to get you the best rates and terms, and not that he or she will. In business and in life I have learned that it is your responsibility to do everything that is necessary to have the right people on your team working with you. This means you must exercise your own due diligence when looking for a professional to advise you. Believe it or not, not everyone is out there looking out for your best interests.

A broker will pull your credit score once and use the information to negotiate with several banks on your behalf. If you personally went from bank to bank searching for a mortgage, each bank would pull your credit report and this might have adverse effects on your credit rating in the future.

Before you commit to a broker, be sure you do your homework. Make sure you are working with someone who is going to put you in the right mortgage. Most importantly, make sure you have asked the right questions before signing on the dotted line.

Jennifer's Story

Good income, smart lady, but poor errors in judgment put her on the wrong financial track.

Jennifer happens to be a good friend of mine who became a client after many years. She purchased her personal life insurance through me and was putting money away annually toward her RRSP.

At 50 years old Jennifer was making good money (approximately $80,000 a year), but she was not in a defined benefit plan with her employer. This meant she would need to find another way to help her through her retirement years.

Jennifer owned her home with about $152,000 remaining after 12 years of paying the mortgage. Not bad — with continued discipline she would be mortgage-free by the time she retires.

I dropped in to see Jennifer over the Christmas holiday to share a glass of wine and see how she was doing. She asked me how my real estate investing and business was coming along, and I told her that things were moving in the right direction, saying I couldn't be more pleased. I then asked how things were going with her. "Let me show you," she said.

Turns out my good friend had made some errors in judgment. She was in a high-interest mortgage at 5.3% with three and a half years remaining on the five-year term. It was taking a considerable amount of money out of her pocket to service the interest at a time when variable interest was as low as 2.25%. She had a line of credit maxed out at $75,000 paying 5% interest. There were two credit card debts, one at $19,800 at 18.9% and the other at $12,400 at 9%. Jennifer was paying more than $3,000 a month to service her accumulated debt. She was paying $1,000 toward her line of credit, $1,000 toward her credit cards, and another $1,100 on her mortgage.

Even though she was putting what seemed to be major dollars toward her debts, it would still take her more than 30 years to pay them all off.

My only response after seeing all this red was, "Wow ... you are in trouble. So let's fix it." Now, I am not a mortgage broker, but I knew she had been handed a raw deal when it came to her mortgage terms. Paying 5.3% at a time when five-year fixed rates were available for approximately 4% to 4.4% was highway robbery no matter how you looked at it!

We did some calculations and decided the best thing for Jennifer to do was to break her mortgage. She would have to pay a penalty, but our calculations showed she would be much better off in the long run.

Jennifer had some equity built into the home, and had done some renovations over the years. We had the house appraised, borrowed 80% of the appraised value, and packaged it into a new mortgage at 2.25%. The 80% borrowed on the appraised value was enough to pay off both credit cards, the penalty for breaking her mortgage, and the line of credit.

Jennifer now had a single item of debt, a mortgage of $252,000. We had reduced her monthly debts to just under $1,200 per month to service the new mortgage.

We also got her into a step mortgage with her lender. A step or matrix mortgage allows increased access to funds from your secured line of credit as you pay down the principal on your mortgage.

With an increasing line of credit at "prime + one" (**prime rate - the interest rate that commercial banks charge their most creditworthy borrowers, like large corporations, set by the bank of Canada**), Jennifer is in a much better position and will likely never get caught up in high-interest credit card payments again.

She has already committed $6,000 to her investment portfolio since taking out the new mortgage, and is attacking the principal on the mortgage by doubling up on her monthly payments to the bank. At this rate she could be totally debt-free in 8.5 years and have an additional $55,000 in her investment account.

Jennifer is, however, turned on by real estate investing and does not plan to pay off her mortgage so soon. Her plan is to pay down the mortgage to the point where she has enough money on her line of credit to purchase a couple of investment properties as part of her retirement income plan.

With a little help and some strategic planning, she is now able to rest easy, as she knows she is on the right track toward a brighter financial future.

Financial Literacy

Jennifer's financial situation didn't occur overnight. For years she had made simple errors that over time became just too much for her to handle. There are millions like Jennifer, who do not see the errors until the results show up in their finances, health, relationships, or businesses. But a few simple habits practised every day have the power to not only turn your life around, but bring success beyond your wildest dreams.

For many years I worked as a personal trainer with the YMCA of Toronto designing programs to get adults in the best shape of their lives. Some of my clients would quit after only a few weeks claiming they were not getting the results they had hoped for.

Individuals with this mindset believe success comes overnight or in a bottle, and are looking for sudden, dramatic changes. But success typically does not come in quantum leaps. It is a gradual process. If we exercise patience and allow time to work its magic we will achieve the results we desire.

When it comes to your financial success you can't afford to make foolish errors with your money. One way to guard against this is to invest in your own financial education. Those who take the time to learn the basics about the world of finance are more informed and make better decisions.

For years I followed the advice of so-called financial planners on how I should invest. They were eager to promote one mutual fund after another, but never seemed to find the time to educate me on why this one was better than another, or provide me with adequate exit strategies to protect my investments.

To compound matters, I was not able to hold them accountable if I lost my money. It really ticked me off when I suffered losses to be told that investing should be for the long run. That might work for some, but I work hard for my money and hate losing it. The last thing I need to hear is some rehearsed line fed to advisors by their companies that investing is for the long run, so we should not be too concerned with occasional losses.

Seeing the flaws in this system, I decided to take matters into my own hands and get my own life insurance and mutual funds licence. Now, I am not advising you to go out and take courses to become a licensed agent, but you do need to take time to read some books and regularly attend seminars to stay informed about what is going on in the marketplace.

You must make your personal finance a priority. It cannot be treated lightly or controlled by the advice of others; believe me, they do not have your best interests at heart. You might not have the time to manage your own portfolio, and that is understandable, but you should at least know the basics so you do not get taken advantage of.

Many approach the topic of personal finance with little regard for how it will shape their future success. Some are content with rolling the dice and hoping they survive the outcome. Don't let that be you. You must have a clear plan for your financial success and be willing to do whatever it takes until you achieve it.

Those who achieve financial success understand that the greatest investment they can make is the one in their own education. Benjamin Franklin had a great quote: "Empty your wallet into your mind and your mind will fill your wallet."

What a profound statement that is! Are you investing in your own personal development? Are you buying books in order to shape your personal outlook on success?

I hear many of you saying, "I can't afford to buy books and spend money on seminars. I can hardly get by as it is." What I can tell you from having gone through the process of changing my life is that no external change will occur for you until you are willing to change your internal blueprint.

What you feed your mind will determine what you manifest on the outside. Your outlook determines your attitude, your attitude determines your actions, and the compound effects of the actions you perform on a regular basis ultimately lead to your success or your failure.

One way to get out of this "stinking thinking" that has kept millions trapped in perpetual servitude is to rethink the above statement by asking,

"How can I find a way to afford the books and seminars?" When you ask the right questions, your subconscious will take on the challenge of finding a solution. When you say "I can't," the creative process shuts down and your subconscious delivers the very thing you expect and nothing more.

What if you are really at rock bottom and can't see a way of coming up with $20 to buy that one book that could unlock the doors to untold treasures? Does this mean there is no hope for you? Of course not, I love buying my own books and being able to read them when I want. Over the years I have been able to put together a very nice library with some terrific authors. But you don't need to have a home library to start unlocking the doors of your creative mind. You can join your local public library and begin the process of reading 10 to 15 pages of a powerful book daily to increase your knowledge and change your philosophy. Books on finance are a must, as well as books on personal development and autobiographies of successful people[15].

Do you know how many people take advantage of this free resource at their local library to increase their knowledge about any topic they could ever want to learn? About 5%! Can you believe that?

Guess what percentage of the world's population control more than 90% of the world's wealth — you guessed right, about 5%. Do you think there might be some slight correlation between reading and success?

So why don't more people join the library? Well, as we have seen before, it is easy to do but also easy not to do.

The late Jim Rohn, one of the most well-known business coaches and personal development leaders said: "You need to read every day; you can miss a meal but not your reading, reading unlocks the doors to your future success."

In leadership we often hear that leaders are readers, but I would like to add *that readers are achievers*. If you are not achieving the success you currently seek, then I would suggest you begin the change process by emptying your wallet into your mind so your mind can fill your wallet.

Billionaire Secrets to Wealth

Some people can clearly afford to be big spenders but have chosen to be frugal and live a simple lifestyle. Might we learn some valuable lessons from their examples and apply it to our own lives? I believe so, and that is why I want to share a bit about the habits and lifestyle of some of the ultra-rich in society.

---

15   Ziglar, Zig. *Over The Top*. Nashville, Tennessee: Thomas Nelson, 1994

Carlos Slim might not be a name you are familiar with, but when it comes to massive success in the world of business and wealth creation he tops the list of those who have their money right. Carlos Slim Helu is a telecom tycoon and billionaire with well-known frugal tendencies. According to the March 7th, 2012 issue of *Forbes* magazine in a piece written by Alan Farnham, Carlos Slim has a net worth of $69 billion[16]. Now that is some serious spending power.

How to Make $1 Billion

Granted, the world's billionaires (all 1,226 of them) as of the writing of this book in March 2012, are in the position of having, quite literally, more money than they can possibly spend, yet some still live well below their means and save money in surprising places. Even non-billionaires like you and me can benefit from taking part in some of these spending tips from our frugal billionaires.

1. *Keep your home simple.* If I were a billionaire, I could afford to live in the most exclusive mansions imaginable and I probably would. When it comes to luxury living, no one does it bigger or better than Microsoft's founder Bill Gates, who owns a sprawling 66,000- square-foot, $147.5 million mansion in Medina, Washington. However, this chapter is about reducing your expenses, and most of us would probably agree that spending $147.5 million on a home is not a wise decision, regardless if you are the 3rd richest man in the world worth a cool $44 billion.

   The good news is that Bill's story is the exception, not the norm. Frugal billionaires like Warren Buffet (2nd on Forbes list with $61 billion) choose to keep it simple. I am not telling you to live as frugally as Buffet, but it is interesting to know that one of the richest men in North America still lives in the five-bedroom house in Omaha, Nebraska, that he purchased in 1957 for $31,500. So why do millions of average income earners in Canada and across the globe continue to bite off more mortgage than they can chew? It could be that many

---

16 Farnham, Alan. ABC News, "Carlos Slim: World's Richest Man Again, Says Forbes." Last modified 03/7/12. Accessed 03/15/12.
   http://abcnews.go.com/blogs/business/2012/03/carlos-slim-worlds-richest-man-again-says Forbes/.

mistakenly equate the size of one's house with their level of personal success.

2. *Use self-powered or public transportation.* Thrifty billionaires, including John Caudwell, David Cheriton, and Chuck Feeney, prefer to walk, bike, or use public transportation when getting around town.

   Certainly these wealthy individuals could afford to take a helicopter to their lunch meetings, or ride in chauffeur-driven Bentleys, but instead they choose to get a little exercise or take advantage of public transportation. Good for the bank account and great for the environment. Again, I am sharing this information to make a point, not to tell you that you can do without the things you have come to rely on. In Canada, we have some very cold winters, and I would rather be nestled in the warmth and comfort of my car than standing at a bus stop. I love the convenience of my car, and although it is not the greatest thing for the environment it is not something I personally plan on giving up.

3. *Buy your clothes off the rack.* While some people, regardless of their net worth, put huge emphasis on wearing designer clothes and shoes, some frugal billionaires decide it's simply not worth the effort or expense. I couldn't agree more. It is absolutely astonishing the amounts people are willing to spend on the latest trend. Those who blow their budget on clothing are often doing so to gain acceptance or put on airs. Some will even delay paying their rent just to have the latest designer outfit that is out of fashion by the time the next season comes around. It is important to look good and dress for success, but there are ways to do that without breaking the bank.

   Ingvar Kamprad, founder of the furniture company IKEA, avoids wearing suits, and John Caudwell, the mobile phone mogul, buys his clothes off the rack instead of spending his wealth on designer clothes. I suggest you follow their example by dressing smart on a budget, and put your money to work where it can return a profit.

4. *Drive a regular car.* While billionaires like Larry Ellison, co-founder and CEO of Oracle, enjoy spending millions on cars, boats, and planes, others remain low-key with their vehicles of choice. You might not know the story of Jim Walton, but

it is well worth reading his biography if you get the chance. Walton is a member of the Wal-Mart clan — you know, Wal-Mart, that little discount store that keeps popping up in a city or town near you. Well, Jim drives a 15-year-old pickup truck and loves it. And Kamprad of IKEA drives a 10-year-old Volvo. I guess there is nothing wrong with my nine-year-old Honda Civic after all. If you are going to keep money in your pocket, the idea is to buy a dependable car and drive it into the ground. No need for a different car every day of the week for these frugal billionaires.

5. *Skip luxury items.* It might surprise some of us, but the world's wealthiest person, Carlos Slim — the one who could spend more than a thousand dollars a minute and not run out of money for 100+ years — does not own a yacht or plane. And many other billionaires have chosen to skip these luxury items. Buffett says, "Most toys are just a pain in the neck."

Key Takeaway

Despite their ability to have anything money can buy, some of the world's billionaires have adopted frugal habits throughout their lives. The jury is out on whether their current outlook is what allowed them to build their empires or whether the building of their empires shaped their philosophy. One thing is for certain, though: we can learn valuable lessons from their examples about the value of a dollar and how to grow our wealth. You might never earn billions or even millions in your lifetime, but regardless of the income you earn, you can adopt their philosophy and find ways to cut your expenses and leave more money in your pocket.

Chapter Four

Protect Your Money

So far we have discussed two fundamental principles for successfully navigating the financial landscape:

1. When we develop the disciplined habit of saving, the universe cooperates with us and provides us with more. Without developing this quality in your character it will be very difficult for people to trust you with more money. The importance of this fundamental principle cannot be overstated; it is the most critical piece to unlocking the financial puzzle of our lives.

2. A properly planned budget can help eliminate the leaks in your spending and move you onto the right financial track. Our inability to delay gratification and limit our wants can have an adverse impact on our financial success, and this fundamental error in judgment is what keeps millions in perpetual servitude.

In short, practising a few simple habits every day could mean the difference between living a life of quiet desperation or a life of gratitude and anticipation.

The third key in the financial fitness blueprint is to *protect your money*. A part of all you earn is yours to keep and this portion of your income should be guarded fiercely.

You probably understand by now that even though errors in your personal outlook may have kept you settling for an average life, money was available to you all the time. Your disciplined approach to saving has yielded a fatter bank account, and putting 10% to 20% aside every month, which seemed impossible a few short months ago, is now an old habit and you no longer worry about money.

As your confidence and your bank account grow, you start thinking of ways to increase the money coming into your life. This feeling is natural (it is not greed), so don't fight it, but you need to get some education about where to put your money or risk losing it all.

One of my goals in writing this book is to help others avoid some of the mistakes I have made along my financial journey, mistakes that are easily avoidable when you have proper coaching and are willing to take immediate action. My mentors have been priceless additions to my circle of influence and have helped to accelerate my progress in all areas of my life. I want you to think of this book as your personal mentor.

Guard your money like a lion

> *Gold clings to the cautious owner, even as it flees the careless owner. The man who seeks the advice of men wise in handling gold, soon learns not to jeopardize his treasure, but to preserve it in safety and to enjoy its consistent increase in contentment.*
>
> —George S. Clason

This quote is from one of my favourite books on finance, *Richest Man in Babylon* by George S. Clason (1926). It is well worth spending an evening to digest Clason's teachings through parables. They outline practical steps for getting your life on the right financial track.

It's interesting to note that the same financial concerns that plagued society in the early 1920s are still ongoing concerns in 2012. Most importantly, the formula for getting one's personal finance on track has not changed. The principles that allowed men and women to create massive wealth throughout history are still being used today to change the lives of millions from ordinary to extraordinary.

Many of us have grown up hearing the maxim "If it ain't broke, don't fix it." Well, the formula for financial success is not broken. It has withstood the test of time and keeps on ticking. All you have to do is follow the path set by those who have achieved financial success and you can duplicate their results.

From my research I have come to understand that gold truly clings to the cautious owner. Not only does it cling, but it tends to come in increasing amounts to those who truly know how to protect it and keep it safe.

But beware! As you start to move your life forward and your finances start to take shape, you will be bombarded with a host of "wonderful" opportunities. You will start hearing how this or that offer is limited to only a select few or how you only have 24 hours to make your decision. *Don't be fooled!* Don't ever make a financial decision without having an exit strategy. Take the time to consult with others more knowledgeable than you in the area in which you are considering investing. Heed my advice, I am speaking from experience. Do your best to avoid throwing good money at bad ideas. As you start to climb the financial success ladder, remember that capital preservation is better than the hope of capital appreciation. *Do not lose your money!*

Eric's Story

I can't overstate the value of a good mentor in helping you elevate your life to the next level. A mentor helps you see your mistakes and keeps you on track to accomplishing your dreams. They will hold you accountable for your actions and expect results, not excuses.

My friend Eric could have certainly used a mentor's counsel before he got involved in what he initially thought was a too-good-to-be-true investment. Unfortunately he was not looking for a mentor, because he figured the opportunity presented to him was a slam-dunk. He trusted the suits at the front of the room with their fancy PowerPoint presentation and rosy projections of guaranteed future income.

Eric was a hard-working colleague of mine who had been a teacher for more than 10 years. He was making good money and had a handle on his finances, but he was ambitious, and wanted to increase his wealth exponentially. He had been getting his taxes done by a big-shot accountant and financial advice from one of the high rollers on Bay Street.

Eric desperately wanted to elevate his financial status and was easily convinced by his advisor to take part in a tax shelter that promised to deliver massive returns on his money when he filed his taxes. In simple terms, he was told that if he gave $10,000 to this particular charity he would receive a tax receipt equaling approximately 1.5 times his donated amount, or $14,000 to 15,000.

He was told there was some risk involved when taking part in any tax shelter, but the organizers felt confident as their charity had never been audited by Canada Revenue Agency (CRA) in more than 12 years. Eric liked the sound of that, and despite growing concern about getting involved, he took the plunge.

He donated $15,000 to this charity and anxiously waited for his tax return. When it finally arrived, Eric couldn't wait to see if what he had been promised was actually true. He opened the envelope and a smile creased his face as he saw a cheque from CRA for $22,000. He could hardly contain himself, and went to the bank to cash the cheque immediately. He was over the moon, and could hardly wait to make another donation the following year. The second year he donated $20,000 and received a cheque for $28,000.

Eric was in financial heaven and felt he had tapped the mother-load of free money. After receiving his second cheque from CRA, he quickly cashed it and decided to do some much-needed renovations on his house. He was enjoying his newly found genie in a bottle and was already considering how much to donate the next year.

But his daydreaming stopped abruptly the day he was notified by CRA of a reassessment of his charitable contributions. Sometime later a second letter came stating that the contributions were being disallowed. Eric was informed that he would be required to repay the entire tax credit that he had received from the CRA for both years.

He felt sick to his stomach. For several weeks he had trouble sleeping, and sorely regretted having jumped into something he had always suspected was too good to be true. When he finally contacted the charity, he was assured this was a normal part of the process and that the CRA was trying to weed out the good charities from the bad.

It is anybody's guess as to how this saga will unfold in the tax courts. But one thing is for certain: Eric could very well be on the hook for $50,000 if the CRA wins its challenge in tax court. "If only I had listened to my gut," he tells me.

Eric's desperate push to accelerate his wealth was based on greed (his own words, not mine). His error in judgment has left him feeling anxious about where to find $50,000 should the test case before the CRA not work out in his favour.

Eric's story isn't unique. There's a tendency for most people to want to increase their wealth exponentially, especially when they start to see their bank balances grow. The thing to remember is that there is no such thing as overnight success when it comes to your finances. Success requires patience and good judgment.

A good friend and mentor of mine once told me that something resembling "overnight success" is indeed possible for those who are disciplined and willing to commit themselves to their dreams, but it usually takes 10 to 15 years of disciplined effort before it happens. This friend has had many successful businesses and is a millionaire many times over, so when he speaks I listen, and you should do the same.

All along, Eric had had an uneasy feeling in his gut about the charity, but had dismissed it. He had felt something was wrong, but wanted desperately not to miss out on an opportunity that could bring back returns five times the average return of the stock market — the kind of return that could set him up nicely for the rest of his life. He needed to ask himself: Is this too good to be true? We all want to succeed financially, and some people unfortunately are enticed to compromise their best judgment.

Who among us would not love to get a 40% - 50% return on our money? At that rate of return your investment dollars would double every 1.8 or 1.4 years respectively! You would never have to worry about money for the rest of your life. When you don't understand the rules of money it is easy to get taken by those promising outrageous returns when you are trying to put your finances in order. Not only are these returns highly unlikely, they are unsustainable for any length of time. When you suspect something is too good to be true, you need to exercise caution and follow your gut. If you are about to make decisions regarding an investment and have difficulty sleeping because of growing concerns, it is probably best to walk away.

Eric's desire for more led him to overlook the third step in the financial fitness blueprint, which is to protect your money. His story is here as a warning to those who have unrealistic expectations for what their money can do when invested.

Stay on track

You have practised the disciplined approach to investing and have followed the 60, 15, 5, 20 formula for wealth creation. Your spending is now in balance and you've learned to reduce the money spent on wants to a manageable 15% while keeping your must-haves or needs to 60%. You feel grateful to be in a position to donate 5% to your favourite charity, and the 20% that you have been putting toward investing has started to grow significantly. You are now tempted to pull money out to live a little.

Don't do it. There is a reason you are following this formula. It is to ensure your future financial success. If you start pulling money from your savings you will not be able to live the life you want throughout your retirement.

It is easy to think there is more than enough when you start watching the power of compounding, but your goal for this portion of your income is to build wealth and leave a legacy. The minute you start taking money out, you lose the discipline and break the habit of saving and investing. This simple mistake can end up costing you thousands in retirement funds because you failed to maximize the power of compounding interest. You need to protect your principal, as it will be the key factor allowing you to take advantage of life's many opportunities.

Let's take a look at the financial mistakes Sean made when he focused on liabilities instead of assets and tapped into his savings account.

Sean had saved a considerable amount of money, and was in the top 5% of income earners. As his bank account grew, so did his appetite for living the good life and travelling. His income was such that he didn't worry about money. He was a successful businessman and felt confident he could always generate more income as needed.

Sean decided he wanted a Porsche. Although he realized this was not the best use of his money, his desire for a luxury sports car was overwhelming. His lack of discipline led to him making a decision that didn't protect his money.

For starters it cost him $160,000. He withdrew a significant amount of money from his nest egg and eliminated it from the power of time and compounding. He did so to purchase a liability that decreased in value.

Let's assume Sean had left that money in an investment account for 10 years earning a return of 10% annually and reinvested the interest. Here is what that money could have done for him.

In year one, Sean would have earned a whopping $16,000 in interest. If he reinvested this $16,000, his investment dollars for year two would be equal to $176,000. At the end of year two, he would have earned an additional $17,600 in interest. That is $16,000 from year one, plus $17,600 in year two, for a total of $33,600 after only two years of investing. At the end of 10 years, Sean's $160,000 would have ballooned to $414,998. The power of time and compounding would have allowed Sean's initial investment to earn more than $250,000 of interest.

Can you afford to give up this kind of future wealth just to satisfy a wish that is not a necessity of life? Two hundred fifty thousand dollars is a hefty price to pay for a car you can only drive during the short Canadian summers.

If you are currently making poor decisions, there is hope for you. I myself have made countless errors in my personal finance over the years, but the key for both you and me is to learn from the errors and resolve to never make them again.

Anyone who goes through life making the same mistakes over and over again will never rise to any notable level of success. Sean understood that the Porsche was a colossal error in judgment. He has since made changes in how he handles his money and weighs everything before he pays. He is committed to spending no more than 50% of his money on his wants and needs combined. The other 50% of his income he now puts toward his investments.

Of course, Sean's situation is far from typical. He has no mortgage and has significant income from his businesses. I would not dare suggest you put 50% of your earnings into investments. The 60, 15, 5, 20 formula for wealth will be more than sufficient to get you financially fit and ensure you live your life by design.

My earlier "Eric" story and this one are examples of poor money judgment that began with the hope of hitting one out of the park. It is very easy to get lured into the many schemes promising instant wealth. In my early years, I too was drawn in. I wanted to make immediate and significant corrections in my family's poor financial health and lacked patience and discipline. My philosophy has since changed significantly, and I am grateful to have met several mentors' kind enough to take me under their wing.

Watch out for Sharks in Suits

I was once invited by a former accountant to attend a business opportunity meeting for a new company. The presentation was very well done, and the guys in suits at the front explained the exhaustive research that had gone into a new product they were manufacturing and the string of companies on a waiting list to have the product delivered to the marketplace.

They talked about the timeline to full-scale production and the positive environmental impact this product would have over its competitors in the market. Everything was ready to go, all except the hundreds of thousands in funding needed to bring this business to life and turn a profit.

The profit projection for each partner based on their investment dollars was clearly presented with bar-graphs, pie-charts, and line-graphs to impress. These profit margins were described as conservative, so everyone was excited. A few questions were asked about the research done, but a strong pitch was made that if we wanted in we had to act now. Not being a seasoned investor or understanding the business model, I relied on the advice of the gentleman who had invited me to the meeting.

That was my first mistake. You see, there was an added incentive for him to have me sign up and put my dollars into this project: he would be making a commission on my investment dollars.

My second mistake was that I did not do any research on the company, the product, or the competition currently in the market.

My third mistake, and probably the most costly, was that I did not ask about an exit strategy or how liquid the investment was should I need my money out in case of an emergency.

I blindly followed the lead of my accountant who, I erroneously believed, was looking out for my best interests. But he was concerned only with bringing in uneducated investors and using his influence to get them to sink their money into this investment. Did it work? You better believe it did. My desire for the instant profits and residual income stream was strong, and I sank a cool $30,000 into this company.

So how did this work out for me? I am sure you can guess by now. Ignorance and greed will bury you. You must do your very best to guard against these character flaws.

Here is the rest of this story. Within a year I received a letter telling me that the two gentlemen trusted to run this limited partnership had stolen money from the partners and the company would be under new management.

Shortly after that, I got another letter asking me for additional funding to keep the company afloat, to avoid my losing the $30,000 I had already invested. I turned additional funds over to the company, because like the other investors I felt another $5,000 to keep the company afloat until it turned a profit was a small price to pay if I could protect my original investment.

After five years, that money has yet to produce any income, and the opportunity cost has been enormous. Just imagine what you could do with $30,000 cash in your hands. It could be a down payment on a $300,000-dollar home, or invested in the stock market and safely returning 6% to 8% annually. What about taking your family on that once-in-a-lifetime trip, or using it as seed money to launch your own business? The possibilities are endless. These are the opportunity costs I have had to absorb because of my ignorance and greed.

By sharing my mistakes with you, it is my hope that you will use my examples as a warning of how not to live your life. You need to become self-sufficient when it comes to creating a financial future for you and your family. Financial literacy should be a priority for each of us. You can't count on your bankers and advisors to always do what is best for you. To think the individual working at the bank is in the best position to give you sound financial advice about your money is an error you just don't want to make.

Your local bank employee is probably swimming in debt like the majority in society, so how can he or she teach you the strategies for financial success? If they personally knew the strategies for creating lasting wealth, chances are you would not find them behind some counter watching the clock waiting to leave work. They are merely employees for the big moneymaking machine ("The Bank") and are in the business of selling products, not creating wealth.

No, you cannot rely on anyone but yourself. To think otherwise will put you in a world of hurt. Take my advice. I have seen the results from both sides of the counter, and the rewards I am currently reaping are far greater than anything my banker or advisor could have done for me. It is up to you to take full responsibility for your finances.

Singles Are Better Than Home Runs

It is easy to be tempted by opportunities that offer the chance to make large sums of money in short periods of time. Friends and relatives who might want the best for you are sometimes guilty of bringing these get-rich-quick schemes to the attention of those who have accumulated a small amount of savings. But is it wise to be roped in by the possibility of larger earnings when your principal may be lost? Of course not, and the examples shared in this chapter are testimonials to that.

True wealth is a process, and just like a vintage bottle of wine that requires years before it is ready, so too is the process for creating lasting wealth.

Consider the man who wins the lottery and overnight becomes an instant millionaire. Doesn't that sound good? "Millionaire"! Yes, many of us would love to win a million or two playing the lottery, and this desire for overnight wealth drives the widespread addiction to playing the lottery. But being rich and being wealthy are two different things. The majority of lottery winners lose all their winnings within a few years.

Why does this happen? Contrary to popular belief, winning the lottery, in itself, does not set you up for life. Most people believe money is the key to wealth, but it is only a part of the equation. To be sure, money is important; but we've seen that it's your personal outlook that leads to one amassing wealth.

To attract wealth into your life, you must grow and change as an individual. When you grow and change from the inside out, your outer world expands, bringing the things you desire most into your life.

Wealth is a state of mind. It is the development of a personal philosophy strong enough to endure the challenges of life. Donald Trump lost billions in the early stages of building his real estate empire, but he was able to make it all back again because he had the correct outlook and believes he is the co-creator of his life. He knows he is the one holding the keys to the financial vaults of life and therefore can have anything he wants.

Those who have achieved wealth know how to make money work for them. They have exercised patience throughout the years and spent time on personal development. They see the world as a reflection of what is developed on the inside and because they focus first on changing themselves from the inside, they are then able to attract abundance into their lives.

The wealthy understand the formula for wealth creation and follow it with precision. They do not gamble or hope for instant riches by playing the lottery. The man who is wealthy understands that true wealth is created by his consistent effort and commitment to something.

If you have ever watched a baseball game, you know that the objective is to score more runs than the opposition by the end of nine innings. Life and your finances are similar: you want to put yourself in the winning position when the game (you're working years) comes to an end.

Baseball is played with speed and grace, and each player has worked on his craft so that he doesn't become a liability to the team. Because players can affect only their own performance, they work tirelessly with coaches and mentors to improve their game. Your personal finances need to be approached with the same dogged determination to succeed. You need to take the coaching necessary, and do all you can to stay at the top of your financial game.

As a youngster growing up I played baseball in a pee-wee league. I must admit I was not very good, but in fairness I never really gave myself a chance to learn the game. What I do remember, however, is the excitement I felt every time I would watch a grand slam or a massive home run on television. This has got to be the most exciting part of the game, and it is why many adults love going to the ball park. But here's the thing. Did you know that the most exciting part of the game (the long ball) is not what accounts for the most runs scored? Sure, it is nice to see the ball jacked out of the park, but if the goal is to win the game then it is not the grand slam or occasional home run that gets the team to the championship year after year.

The majority of runs scored are due to the *singles and doubles* and a team's ability to protect their lead with stellar defensive plays. Yes, the home-run ball is terrific to watch and often gets the fans on their feet, but it pales in comparison to the singles, doubles, and excellent defense that often go unnoticed.

Babe Ruth was one of the greatest sluggers of all time. He could hit that ball out the park like no one before or since. Everyone remembers the Babe for his batting prowess, but few remember that he struck out more than any other player in the league. Everyone cheers at the home runs, but what about the 8 out of 10 times you swing and miss? Would you be comfortable with that batting average in your personal finances? I doubt it. It's a sure recipe for financial disaster, and yet so many people continue to chase this fantasy and gamble with their future.

If you are going to succeed financially you need to follow the examples of winning World Series champions. Be disciplined at the plate and wait for the pitches you can comfortably handle. Don't swing for everything in hope of hitting one out of the park. Three singles and a double will score more runs for you than a massive home run with no runners on base.

Remember that the goal is to make contact with the ball consistently and get safely to first base. If you swing for every pitch, you are bound to strike out frequently, which will have an adverse effect on your financial health. Once you have scored a few runs, you need to continue exercising patience at the plate and dig down defensively to protect your investments and your profits.

If you are able to follow this principle of protecting your principal and staying disciplined at the plate, you are ready for the next stage in your financial fitness blueprint. Chapter Five will outline how to invest the singles and doubles so your runs multiply exponentially. We will put your money to work and take advantage of the power of time and compounding.

Chapter Five

Put Your Money to Work

You have learned that wealth must first be created in the mind before it can ever materialize in your life. You have practised the disciplined habit of saving/investing and committed the minimum 10% to your future wealth or 20% if you want to accelerate the process. You have learned how to delay gratification and reduce your expenditures. You understand that capital preservation is more important than capital appreciation, and that you should do all you can to protect your money. You have also learned that chasing huge returns is the same as throwing good money after bad and that singles are definitely better than home runs when it comes to building lasting wealth.

These principles are the building blocks needed to attract more into your life. The universe is unfolding as it should, and in order to be trusted with more you must be able to demonstrate you can successfully handle small amounts of cash before the big money comes rolling in.

For many years I failed to understand this simple law of money. My belief was rooted in ignorance. I thought those who had money were lucky in business, had won significant money in the lottery, or were born into wealthy families. I had tremendous difficulty making the connection to a simple formula that if followed would open up the vault to untold riches.

How is your thinking? Is it keeping you from believing you can achieve above average results in your financial life, or do you think being average is your destiny? I am here to tell you that whatever you truly believe for yourself is exactly what you will get. The mind attracts to you that which you focus on. If you believe you can't, then it is very probable that you will not turn on the creative processes needed to show you how it can be done.

Learn to take that destructive word — can't — out of your vocabulary and replace it with; *How can I?* How can I create the life that I truly desire for myself and my family? How can I develop the skills needed to elevate my life? How can I navigate the current financial landscape and build a financial fortress around me that can never be penetrated?

When you ask yourself *'How can I?'* Your subconscious mind goes to work to find the answers. Be prepared to write down the answers, as they will often come without warning. There is a saying that the universe loves speed, so write down the thoughts that come to you or risk losing them forever.

Once you have written them down, you need to evaluate what your subconscious has revealed and take action on the many creative ideas that come your way. Fail to act and nothing happens. There is no magic formula for success. Thoughts without action have no life. If you are ready to take your life to the next level, you need to continue reading. The second part of this book will show you the magic of what can happen if you are disciplined and follow the first four steps in the financial fitness blueprint.

It is now time to apply what you have learned and put your money to work in order to increase your wealth.

It is certainly a wonderful feeling to watch your money accumulate. However, if you take pleasure in putting your money under your mattress where it earns no income, you clearly do not understand how money works. The income you earn is just the beginning of your wealth. By itself it is not enough to bring you financial freedom. You must put your money to work where it can earn an income and multiply.

One of the great things about money is that it never sleeps. It doesn't eat or need time off because of illness. Money doesn't complain about the working conditions. Money will work tirelessly for you. In fact, it is willing to slave day and night for you, all you need to do is put it to work and stand back.

One caveat here: you have to exercise due diligence before putting your money to work. Failing to spend sufficient time in this key area could prove extremely costly.

Don't expect your money to do much before it has had the chance to build up to the task. Your money will increase rapidly over time when making reasonable returns. Don't try to force it to produce unreasonable profits. Having too great an expectation of the type of job your money can do might leave your principal depleted and unable to work for you in the future. Before you can expect your money to move mountains you will need to make sure it builds up its strength by working at less demanding jobs in extremely safe environments. As the days, weeks, months, and years go by, it will start to expand in its capacity to handle bigger projects safely. This expansion, and increased muscle power developed through patience, will prepare your money to do the heavy lifting that can multiply your wealth many times over.

As a green (unseasoned) investor, I put my money to work in some really horrible working conditions. I expected my money to lift mighty loads in search of a huge payday, even before it had the maturity and physical capacity to do so. The end result was depletion of my funds and the inability to take advantage of suitable work when opportunities presented themselves. But this doesn't have to be your story; all you have to do is learn from my example. Let my story serve as a warning of how not to invest.

There is another story more powerful than mine that I wish to share with you now. It gives a classic example of what can happen when we get greedy. The sad thing about this story is that every word of it is true.

How not to live your life

This past summer I had the pleasure of sitting down with a dear friend for dinner and a conversation. The dinner was delicious, but it paled in comparison to the things I learned during our conversation. My friend is blessed, just like you and I, and has lived a rich and rewarding life. She embraces the philosophies being taught in this book and has invested wisely over the years in order to create a financially fit future for herself and her family.

We were enjoying a glass of wine after dinner, and the conversation turned to wealth and how to create your life by design. At this point my friend shared the most remarkable story of "how not to live your life" I have ever heard, the true story of a woman who has accumulated millions but nevertheless lives in poverty and misery. With my friend's permission I now share it with you to serve as a *warning* — not an *example*.

Rachel's Story

Picture a young bride, Rachel, at 20 buying her first home with her wonderful husband. Over the next two decades she saves every dime, and by the age of 40 has accumulated more than a million dollars! Rachel clearly understands rule number one of wealth creation — **pay yourself first** — but look what happens next.

At 40 and now a millionaire, Rachel turns the money over to her husband, who proceeds to lose the entire million on a bad investment. It seems rule number four for wealth creation — **protect your principal** — was not taught to either one of this unfortunate couple.

Not surprisingly, the marriage rapidly deteriorates. Yet Rachel, determined to create wealth for herself, begins to save every penny she makes. Meanwhile, her husband is approached by a friend, who apparently knew nothing of what had happened, and is given money to invest. This time, instead of investing it, the husband just pockets the money and tells the friend the investment had been a bad one. He is taken to court and loses. He declares bankruptcy and legally divorces his wife so as not to lose his house.

Well, Rachel is now 62 and, amazingly, once again a millionaire. And yet she is actually poor.

Why? She is in a loveless relationship with the same man she married 40 years ago (though they are legally divorced). Rachel's desire to create wealth led her to hoard every last dime she could get her hands on; but today her money is hidden in her home, not even in a bank account — because she doesn't want her husband to know how much she has.

Seems hard to believe that one could accumulate that much money over a 20-year period and still be considered poor, doesn't it? Rule number three for wealth creation — put your money to work. Rachel has no concept of what she is doing with her money and has demonstrated this again and again.

So How Did She Become a Millionaire?

During her 40 years of marriage, Rachel was a kept woman never having to pay any of the household bills or the mortgage. She raised three children in her home but no money was ever spent on renovating the home so her children could have a space to play as they grew up.

In fact, the unfinished basement from 40 years ago still serves as a reminder to how miserable an existence she has led. Rachel missed the most important rule of all, *give and you shall receive.* This important rule will be covered in depth in a few chapters. Those who understand and follow this law often find themselves in the company of those considered lucky by the rest of society.

The Love of Money

Rachel's is a tragic story of how not to live your life. Let it serve as a warning that the love of money is truly the root of all evil. Your goal is to have money be a servant for you, and not the other way around. Otherwise money will consume your life for all the wrong reasons. Money has the power to dramatically improve your life and that of those around you, but you must be very careful that your pursuit of the green stuff doesn't cause you to miss out on the important things money just cannot buy.

Here was a woman who had accumulated millions during the course of her life, yet failed miserably in putting it to work to enrich her life and the lives of others. I would even hesitate to call her a millionaire, for the simple reason that in order to attract millions into your life you need to grow from the inside out. Rachel had done nothing of the sort: to hoard cash and never extend your hand to assist others is a poverty mindset, and you will never be trusted with more. Money is attracted to those who give with a willing heart and are money-conscious. Poverty will strike those who are poverty-conscious, fearful, and greedy.

I am sure there will be another chapter to Rachel's story. But I don't believe there will be a happy ending. You have to become more to have more, and unfortunately it seems Rachel has still not finished grade school when it comes to personal development.

In life we can learn valuable lessons from the mistakes we make or from those made by others. If you are on the path to creating a financially fit future, make sure you avoid the mistakes made by Rachel. Take her example as a warning. If you follow the rules of money outlined above and develop harmonious relationships with others, perhaps your life might one day be used as an example for others to follow.

It's not what you make

Growing up in the Ontario Housing communities taught me many valuable lessons about life. I learned how important having clearly defined goals are in moving forward in life. For me getting out of Ontario Housing was definitely a goal that I had set for myself, and I made sure I associated with others who had the same dreams for a better life.

At the end of my junior high school year at Lawrence Heights, I did all I could to get into a high school outside my area. The high school that served my community had failed miserably in preparing the majority of its students for postsecondary education. Many students dropped out and turned to a life of drugs and mediocrity, and I couldn't see that for my life. So I searched and knocked on doors, because I was determined to get out. My search for a better start took me 40 minutes away by bus to a school called Oakwood Collegiate. This was to be one of the best decisions of my young life.

Another lesson learned growing up in Ontario Housing is that your circumstances, regardless of how bleak they are, can always be improved with dogged persistence and determination if your will is strong enough. Remember, if you are going through some tough times right now, they have not come to stay, they will pass. Just keep on moving and taking positive actions on a daily basis and you will be amazed how your life turns out.

Growing up was not easy. There was no storybook ending waiting for us, and we knew it. But I learned to be grateful for what we had, and to never take things for granted. These values were instilled by my mother, who always dreamed of a better life for herself and her children. She taught me the value of going after a thing with faith and determination, and I am forever grateful for her teachings.

Many of life's lessons were taught to me by my mother on the way to and from her job. She had purchased a car during my last year of high school, and I became her private chauffer on the weekends. Before buying the car, my mother had told me to go get my licence. "Why? We don't even have a car," I objected. "Go get your licence," was all she said. If you knew my mother you would understand why there was no other option but to do as she ordered.

A few weeks later my mom came home in a brand-new Chrysler. I was dumbfounded. How the heck could she afford a car on what she made working as a healthcare aide. It didn't make sense. But to my mom it made a lot of sense, because she lived her life seeing things not only as they were, but as they might become. She wanted more, and kept that goal at the forefront of her mind. Despite her low wages, she disciplined herself to do what was necessary to purchase her car.

So why am I sharing this with you? First, be grateful for where you are while in the pursuit of more. You cannot take anything in your life for granted. We often don't know the true value of something until it is taken from us. The mere fact that you are able to purchase this book (thank you) puts you in a better position than 90% of the world's population. So we need to be grateful for what we have and also pursue more.

The second takeaway is that your wealth has more to do with the simple habits you practise daily than with how much you earn. If you surveyed the general population, most would tell you they want to accumulate wealth. Further, they would say that they want enough money to buy what they want, when they want it, and to live life without restrictions. Unfortunately, many would also equate wealth with the amount of money they make, and because they can't see themselves as the founder of a company or the CEO, they consider wealth a pipe dream.

It isn't the income you make that determines your wealth. Yes, lots of money certainly helps, but the most important thing is what you do with it. Hundreds of thousands of people around the world earn six-figure incomes or more and are still just getting by.

They work hard, live in beautiful homes, drive fancy cars, and are the envy of their friends. But when you strip it all away, they are a heartbeat from financial ruin. They are not smart with their money and would rather spend it today on instant gratification. This simple mistake will keep them working long into their "golden" years.

Someone making an average or above-average salary can quickly outpace your six-figure income earner in building lasting wealth if they follow the laws of money. The time tested formula is simple. The key to wealth, regardless of income, is to invest your money where your principal is safe, and your money can grow. Parking your money in a regular bank account that pays little to no interest is almost as bad as putting your money under your mattress — for the simple reason that if your house should burn down at least it would be safe in the bank.

There is no shortcut to wealth. More importantly, your investments have to return a reasonable income in order to grow. Holding your hard-earned dollars in a zero-interest account will keep you in perpetual servitude and assure lean years in your retirement. It is too easy to get duped into believing that as long as your money is safe you will be all right. Nothing is more damaging to your financial future.

If your money is not invested where it brings you a decent return on a yearly basis, the passage of time and inflation will eventually erode your funds. One thousand dollars today will not have the same buying power ten years from now. The only way to increase the buying power of your money, or even maintain it, is by investing it where the return on your money can outpace the rate of inflation. Those who understand this, and begin early, have a much better chance of creating lasting wealth than the six-figure-income earner spending everything on immediate gratification.

This country was built on the imagination, drive, and determination of men and women who wanted more for their lives. They understood the importance of a few simple habits practised every day. History books are filled with the biographies of those who have reaped massive rewards through the development of the right outlook.

Building blocks for success

Most people fail to achieve success in their lives because they lack the discipline needed to stick with a plan for the length of time needed to achieve success. They want things to happen quickly, and if they don't see immediate results they move on to what they assume to be the next-best thing.

Unfortunately, the next-best thing doesn't work quickly enough, and they soon walk away in search of the next unreasonable expectation. They never take the time to study successful people. If they did, they would come to understand the concept that results come last. It takes years of consistently following a few simple habits on a daily basis before the results of your efforts show themselves.

Likewise it can often take a lifetime before you realize your errors have robbed you of the good life. Please understand that when I speak of success I am not speaking just of the money game, but in all areas of your life — your spiritual growth, your professional career, your relationship, your physical fitness, and so on.

Besides having a passion for teaching about finance, I am passionate about my physical fitness. Without your health you have nothing, so it should never be taken for granted. No amount of money can provide comfort and satisfaction if your health is seriously compromised.

I bring up this topic to illustrate that the same formula used for achieving success in your physical fitness is needed to bring you success in all areas of your life, including your financial health.

If you are physically fit it is likely that you followed a few simple habits on a daily basis when it came to your health. Over time your disciplined habits allowed you to achieve the results you were after. It is also very likely you have been at the fitness game for quite some time, and although you might have had your doubts, you stuck with the program because you had clear goals and a plan to get there.

So how did you get in such good shape, and what caused you to commit to your goals even when the pull of friends and family had you second-guessing yourself? Perhaps it all started when you woke up one day and had finally had it with the pathetic condition you were in.

Rolling out of bed after yet another sleepless night, you looked in the mirror and felt totally disgusted at what you saw. Enough! I've had it. I have no muscle tone and can't even find the energy to run up a flight of stairs without pausing to catch my breath. If I don't do something about this right now, I am going to have serious health problems when I get older. Many of my friends are enjoying good health, so why can't I?

You joined a gym and gladly signed up for a physical assessment from one of the trained staff, reasoning that if you've been doing it wrong all your life, you will have to do something different to get a different result. You and your trainer discussed your long-term and short-term goals, and together you put a plan together that you felt you could commit to.

The initial workout was easy enough, and you felt your trainer had been underestimating your ability. However, he cautioned you to go slow and ease into your new habit so your body could adjust to the new demands. He told stories of people trying to do more than they were ready for because they wanted results overnight, and who often ended up getting hurt, or simply quit because they learned the results they wanted weren't going to come easy.

You realized you would need to have patience and stay focused on your long-term goals if you were going to be successful. Your trainer told you not to get discouraged if you didn't notice significant changes in the first few months. He explained that your body would get stronger every day and that your cardio would improve, but that the changes would be too small for you to notice. He urged you to have faith and stay disciplined, and assured you that the cumulative effects of your daily habits would bring the results you desired.

So you followed the advice of your trainer and got yourself to the gym three or four times a week. In the beginning it was hard, and many days you felt like skipping, but you stuck with it and it became part of your daily routine. Several months passed, and you felt stronger and had more energy throughout the day. However, you were concerned, because you were not seeing any changes in your body.

Some of the new friends you made at the gym seemed to be in excellent shape, and you asked them what you might be doing wrong.

They told you about their eating habits and how you have to be careful what you put into your body. It is one thing to come to the gym and work out regularly but going to McDonald's regularly will erase the good work you have been doing in the gym. Why didn't you recognize this before? You decided to start eating more fruits and vegetables and stay away from the fast-food restaurants.

With your better eating habits you definitely started to notice a difference in your body. But the real proof of lasting change was when you ran into a friend you had not seen for several months. The first thing out of your friend's mouth was a compliment about how great you looked. "Are you working out, how long and where?" she asked. You beamed. The encounter provided more fuel to your already burning passion, and you became more committed than ever.

As your fitness level increased you started reading more articles on how to maintain and improve your health. Pretty soon you became known to others in the gym as the fitness guy. People came to ask you questions on how to get their "six-pack" or the best exercise for the upper pectorals. You felt great because the more you shared the better understanding you had about the subject yourself.

It has now been several decades since you made the commitment to get your health on track, and the results have been priceless. You are on top of the world. You've expanded your association with others who also have a passion for health and living life to the fullest. Your excellent health has allowed you to travel the world on wilderness tours and even climb mountains. You are the envy of your family and neighbours when they hear the many stories you bring back from your expeditions around the world.

They too could have been living the good life, if they had been willing to pay the price up front. Instead they settled for what was easy at the time, sleeping in, taking their health for granted, not watching what they ate, and avoiding the gym like the plague. Their errors in judgment brought them down the failure curve, robbing them of the quality of life at the time they needed it the most.

The sad thing is that it could have easily been avoided by following the formula in this book, and heeding the advice and information given in countless other works on the topic. What would it cost you, a few dollars? Isn't that a small price to pay for what could possibly unlock the doors to unlimited future success?

Whatever you decide to do after reading this book, don't let that be you. The physical fitness example above illustrates that success comes to those who have a clear plan and vision for their lives. If you apply the principles above to your financial life and commit to doing the seemingly insignificant things on a daily basis, you will achieve financial fitness.

Maximize your returns

The purpose of investing is to ensure a reasonable return on your money; otherwise why invest? It makes absolutely no sense to me why so many people would be content with parking their money in a money market or savings account that pays little to no interest. They have developed the disciplined habit of saving, and that is great, but it is only one piece of the puzzle. The most important piece is that your money must grow.

Investing successfully does involve some risk, but there is a big difference between accepting risk and taking risks with your money. Maybe you believe looking for better returns outside of GICs and money market accounts is just too risky. But here is what you need to understand: without some level of risk you cannot hope to achieve much.

As a real estate investor, I have come to realize that there are three types of investors. All three are usually hardworking, family-oriented individuals who want to do more for their communities and leave a legacy. And they will all tell you that financial freedom would bring tremendous satisfaction to their lives.

But this is usually where the similarities end. It is one thing to claim you want financial freedom, and quite another thing to read the books, attend the classes, and set your sails in order to change your outlook and build your life by design.

I have spent countless hours with people who are looking for an investment that will provide absolute safety for their principal and yet generate high returns to grow their wealth. Sadly, this group is delusional. In life, and in investing, there can be no sure thing. Again, by risk I do not mean risky. We can eliminate most investment risk by taking the time to educate ourselves and increase our financial IQ.

If you turn on your television, the news channels are abuzz with the latest developments in the Eurozone and the coming financial collapse. Yet, despite this, millions around the world continue to successfully invest their money and are getting returns that consistently beat the markets. Why is that? Could it be they aren't swayed by popular sentiment or TV hype? Remember, if you are going to get great results in any area of your life, you cannot continue to do what the majority of people around you are doing. Sadly, only about 5% of the population truly understands this.

Seriously, take a close look at what has been fed to the majority of us by our media outlets and our banks. The key buzzword is "safety" for your capital, and our banks have marketed this so successfully that millions flock to Certificates of Deposit (CDs) and Guaranteed Investment Certificates (GICs) like flies to honey. To be sure, you cannot overlook the importance of safety, but the only thing a GIC guarantees is that your purchasing power will be eroded by time and inflation.

Let's look at an example. We'll use our friend Rachel whom we spoke about earlier in this chapter.

Rachel works hard and has accumulated $300,000 in a non-registered GIC that returns 4% — not bad. She has been extremely disciplined in her saving habits and has resisted all temptation to part with her money. Let us assume that Rachel's income has her in one of the top tax brackets and her marginal tax rate is 43% (**marginal tax rate is the rate of interest paid on earned income; the higher your earned income the higher your marginal tax rate**). Let us also assume that inflation is running at 2.3%, which is quite reasonable as we come to the end of the first quarter of 2012.

GIC income	=	**$300,000 @ 4% = $12,000**
Taxes at 43%	=	**$5,160**
Net return	=	**$6,840**

If we take Rachel's net return of $6,840 and divide it by the $300,000 invested, we get a true return of 2.28% or 2.3%.

How did she do? Did she make any progress? Did her money grow for her? Of course not; if you take our 2.3% inflation rate into account, Rachel had a real return on her money of exactly zero percent.

To me that is a recipe for disaster. If you have that much money in your pocket, I suggest you put it to work where the true return on your money is high enough to outstrip the rate of inflation. Keeping pace with inflation is not investing. Your money is safe but it is not growing.

As an eternal optimist, I always try to look on the positive side of things. Yes, our economy has tanked, and there continue to be uncertainty regarding the financial future of entire countries. Yet, despite all this global uncertainty, millions of people around the world continue to safely and successfully invest their money with returns that consistently beat the markets. These individuals understand that capital preservation is still better than the hope of capital appreciation, and will do what is necessary to guard their principal against unnecessary loss. However, they have embraced the philosophy taught by Robert Kyosaki[17] that they should profit when they buy and when they sell. They will accept risk in order to grow their money, but that does not mean their investments are risky.

As I have said, I am not a fan of guaranteed investment certificates (GICs) because they are not the best instruments for growing your wealth. If you are in your early 20s and have 30 or 40 years of your working life ahead of you, you have to find something better to do with your money. Parking your precious dollars in a GIC will not bring you the kinds of returns that will allow you to live a comfortable life in your retirement.

However, if you are within 10 years of your retirement, GICs, bonds, and CDs are definitely investment products worth considering. With only a few years to go before retirement, you have to secure your principal, it is no time to try and be a hero and put all your money into equities. The market can be merciless in the punishment it dishes out to unsuspecting investors who believe they have a foolproof strategy for beating the markets. Remember, "A fool and his money are soon parted," and there is no bigger fool than the one who believes he or she can game the stock market and claim massive returns. The market always wins. Trust me I have learned the hard way.

What is the alternative? Can we achieve financial success without high risk to our capital? I am here to tell you it is possible. I know, because others have done it and so can you. You see, on a physiological level there is absolutely no difference between those who are financially successfully and those who aren't. We all have the same desires, suffer the same setbacks, and bleed when we get cut.

---

17 *Kiyosaki, Robert, and Sharon Lechter. Rich Dad Poor Dad. Business Plus, 2000.*

So what is it? What makes one group so successful and the other not? The real answer can be found in how they think. Those who achieve financial freedom usually go through a rebirth and change from the inside out (what I have been referring to throughout this book as your "personal outlook"). Successful people have a prosperity mindset. Psychologically they are wired differently. They don't believe in luck, they believe in self-development and personal growth. They realize that opportunities are around them all the time, and put themselves in a position to take advantage of these opportunities.

This group is not looking for safety. To be sure, they want to protect their capital like everyone else, but their level of education and sophistication allows them to avoid speculative investments and grow their wealth through the application of "slight-edge principles" — doing daily the seemingly insignificant things that might not show big results in one month or even one year, but over the years often lead to outstanding benefits.

So what group do you belong to? Are you looking for safety or freedom? Take some time to reflect on that question. You can continue to go the safety route marketed to the masses, or you can find the courage to step outside your comfort zone and take the road less travelled in order to blaze your own trail.

Over the years I have come to discover that doing what is easy will make your life hard but doing what is hard will make your life easy. My advice would be to do what is hard while you are young and have the energy and vitality to put in the time and hard work. If you put it off, there is no guarantee that you are going to get around to it or that you will have the energy. Most importantly, you might find yourself running short on time, and the price to be paid at that late stage of your life is far greater than you can afford.

As a real estate investor and a financial fitness trainer, I don't put much stock in playing it safe by investing in GICs and money market accounts (unless of course you are just a few years from retirement). You need to go after what you want, and if financial fitness is your true desire, you have to begin by changing your mindset.

The Snowball Effect

In this chapter we have covered the importance of putting your money to work in order to get maximum returns, and we will expand on this again before closing the chapter. In life there is a tendency for the majority of us to ease up on the gas pedal the moment we start to see some level of success.

One reason for this is that many people want to be accepted by their family and friends, and feel they will be judged or criticized by the very people they crave acceptance from should they become too successful. These individuals actually fear becoming too successful, and they will often lower their standards and settle for mediocre achievements in order not to alienate others.

Another reason is that the majority in society still operate from a flawed philosophy when it comes to what they believe they deserve. This leads them to find ways of sabotaging the very thing they have been trying to create in their lives.

You need to understand that the creation of your magnificent life is totally your responsibility. You cannot change your past, what's done is done; but you have 100% control of how your future plays out — and for that you should be very excited. Too many people live their lives trying to please this or that person. Their self-worth often hinges on feeling accepted by friends and family members. Yes, it is great when family and friends support our initiatives, it provides additional spark for us to achieve our goals. But when you know without a doubt that eating the apple every day instead of the chocolate bar, or reducing your expenses and investing your money, will elevate your life and bring you success, you must act and develop the habits required. You can't sit around day after day hoping others will give you the go-ahead. Sitting and waiting for acceptance often leads to the *law of diminishing intent.*

You know that law, don't you? You have the best intentions to take a financial literacy course to learn about real estate investing in order to secure your financial future. Or maybe it is to get off your butt and back into the gym to reclaim your magnificent health that has gone bust over the years. But along comes your friend who loves you and wants the best for you. He or she thinks joining the gym is a great idea, and would like to join also so you can get back into shape together. Unfortunately that person does not have the money at the moment, and urges you to wait.

Maybe you share your idea about investing in real estate to build a residual stream of income so you can retire well, only to hear that it is not the right time to invest and that real estate investing is risky. So you decide to wait until your friends, or perhaps family members, are ready to join you.

Pretty soon, weeks and months go by, and with the passing of each day your intention withers away. The law of diminishing intent has crept up to steal your dream because you failed to act. True, your friends and family might really be concerned about your safety in the marketplace, but it is also possible that they want to keep you grounded so you don't spread your wings and fly. Why, because it might remind them that they could have done the same.

Here is my advice. Let others live small lives, not you; if they don't have the vision for a better future, too bad. Don't let that stop you from creating the life you deserve. Get rid of negative thoughts that clutter your mind and surround yourself with people who will encourage you to stretch for the big dreams that are often stored on the top shelf of life.

You deserve to be wealthy, you deserve to have a great career, and you deserve to be in excellent health and most of all you deserve the best life has to offer. If you have done honest work to achieve your success, it is the universe that will reward you for your efforts.

Momentum

If you don't allow yourself to fall victim to the law of diminishing intent or give up on your dreams when success starts to come your way, you won't believe the incredible results that lie just around the bend.

In one of his seminars Zig Ziglar spoke of the importance of financial fitness. He said money is not the most important thing, but it ranks right up there next to oxygen. Now you might not have the same point of view, but you must admit that having money provides you with far more options than not having it.

In my early years I told myself that money wasn't important and that I just wanted to earn enough to get by, and guess what? That is exactly what happened. I got just enough to get by. How pitiful an existence, knowing I had the potential to create as much as humanly possible for my life, but tapped out at just enough.

But one day I found someone who took an interest in me and schooled me on the importance of changing my personal outlook. Once I had made those changes and started taking action, my life began to change dramatically and it has never been the same.

So far in the blueprint, I have shared some key steps needed to build a solid foundation. It's now time to reveal one of the most important lessons in this book. Once you get it, soak it all in, and apply it to your finances; the results will be staggering.

You may want to highlight this section for future reference, as this is where the magic of wealth creation starts to gather momentum. Here is the simplified point to the lesson I am about to share.

Do not eat the fruits of your early labour, reinvest them in order to build momentum and have your harvest multiply in size, year after year.

I can already hear you saying "Why should I not enjoy my fruits, especially when I have worked hard and followed the disciplines outlined so far?" You certainly have a point: life is to be lived to the fullest, and you can't devote your entire life to the accumulation of assets. You need to play and have some fun along the journey. But if you eat too much of the fruits of your labour too soon, you will rob yourself of the momentum needed to build a financial moat around you and your family.

Your methodical approach of delaying early gratification and reinvesting your earnings will, through the power of time and compounding, allow you to produce a harvest that will serve you well in your retirement years and in some cases for generations to come. Then you can eat to your heart's content and enjoy many rich banquets without regret.

I believe the analogy of sowing and reaping is quite accurate. You want to build your wealth by taking advantage of momentum, and the only real way to do that is to reinvest the income earned from your investments so time and compounding have the opportunity to work for you.

I understand that we can't take it with us and that we need to have some fun along the way. But if you are serious about escaping a mediocre life, you cannot continue to do foolish things with your money.

Wealth requires patience and a change in your personal outlook. You have to be willing to pay the price up front, and that price is to live below your means for a time and invest your money wisely.

This doesn't mean giving up all of life's simple pleasures. But it does mean following the budget you outlined in the earlier chapter and having the discipline and courage needed to go after your financial goals. Your reward will be to escape the rat race, and to leave behind a legacy for generations to come.

Chapter Six

Income Protection

Whether you are successful or not, whether you live with regret or are happy with the way your life has turned out, can often be traced back to the outlook you hold. As I reflect on my life and the results achieved thus far, I can't help but wonder how different my life would be if my current philosophies had been adopted in my teens.

Like so many young adults, I didn't have a clue where my life was headed. I simply lived for the moment and followed the lead of others in my immediate community.

One person I really admired was my brother Clive. Clive was a sharp dresser and a gifted communicator who could win you over any day of the week. His gift of the gab and smart fashion sense went over really well with the ladies. He was the consummate ladies' man – maybe that's why I tried to emulate him so much.

When it came to dressing for a night out, my brother had no equal. So I took my cue from him, and will never forget the night he helped me prepare for a wedding I was to attend in Peterborough.

I got home early that Saturday afternoon after renting a nice little sport car for my evening out. As I pulled up, my brother immediately fell in love with the car and went out to rent one for his night out with friends. Although my brother was four years older than me, he had just gotten his licence a week earlier. To say he was excited about being able to finally drive would be an understatement. He was beaming with anticipation.

That evening I had difficulty deciding what to wear, and Clive stepped in to give his expert touch. I looked sharp and my date Yvonne really appreciated it. The wedding was beautiful and we had a great time at the reception.

When we started back for home around midnight, the roads were a complete mess. A huge blanket of snow had fallen in a few short hours, bringing traffic on the side streets to a crawl. Fortunately, the highways were a little better and we made decent time. When we got home my brother hadn't arrived yet, so we went to bed for the night. At 4 a.m. I was awoken by the worst phone call of my life.

It was the police, telling me my brother had been in an accident. They couldn't give me details as the doctors were still running tests. When I finally got to the hospital, I was taken into a room by a team of doctors and given the news that my brother had been killed in a car crash. I couldn't believe what I was hearing. On the way to the hospital, the thought of my brother's death had never even crossed my mind, and here I was about to identify his body.

I had no words to express how I felt as my girlfriend sat with me trying to console me. I was now the only male in my family, and charged with the duty of calling my sisters, uncles, and my mother. How was I going to break this to my mother, who had buried our grandmother only five months earlier? That was my biggest question, and one I wrestled with for some time. In the end the entire family was notified, and one by one they made their way to the hospital.

That very dark period was just the beginning of a series of negative events that would eventually alter the way I lived my life. So why am I sharing this particular story with you? Why am I exposing pieces of my life that seem to have nothing to do with the topic of this chapter? The simple truth is that it has everything to do with it. My brother's death, along with the death of my uncle three months later, opened my eyes to the importance of establishing a solid foundation to protect your family should your number be called early for the big mansion in the sky.

At 25 years my brother had lived a carefree life, and although he had a child, he had given very little thought to his financial future or the protection of his family with basic life insurance. I guess at 25 we all think the same. I was certainly no different.

After my brother's death I started to see how grossly underprepared we were to handle this unfortunate event. As a family we had nothing saved because we knew nothing about how money worked. It was a very sobering time, and quite embarrassing for me to watch the church taking up collections to help us pay for his funeral. I realized something was very wrong with this picture and vowed never to let this happen to us again.

You might not see the value of owning life insurance. You might, like many, consider it a big waste of money and prefer to take your chances with the roll of the dice. Well, take it from me, life insurance is a basic need that you can't afford to do without. It ought to be the foundation of your financial blueprint, since it ensures that, should you be called home prematurely, you have set things in place to protect your family and give them a hand up in your absence.

What is surprising to me is how easily we are able to accept being out of pocket to the tune of hundreds of dollars per month for car insurance but not for life insurance. It is illegal to drive without car insurance and that is probably the only reason most people take out the coverage. But just because life insurance is not mandatory doesn't mean it shouldn't be an important piece of your financial plan. Many people have grown up with misplaced values favouring material things instead of what really matters, our lives and families.

Think about this for a minute. How much is your average eight-year-old car worth, regardless of make and model? Let's say $10,000 to $15,000 tops. One might expect the average driver to be paying insurance of about $120.00 to $150.00 a month for the privilege of driving this car.

Now if I asked you to put a dollar value on your life, would you be able to? I am quite certain that you believe your life is actually priceless. So why is it that more than 40% of the population put more value on insuring a $15,000-dollar car than buying protection to ensure their families' financial success? I believe the word is selfishness, plain and simple. Don't get me wrong: insurance is not for everyone and many have created enough financial security that their family would not suffer should they pass on. But the majority of people are not in that position. Are you?

A story on the November 24th issue of Canada Newswire by Meghan Thomas revealed that 31% of Canadians in a poll conducted by TD Insurance Risky Business did not have life insurance, and 40% of them didn't believe it was needed[18]. That is an alarming statistic, especially for the many families depending on the income of one or both parents just to survive today.

---

18   Thomas, Meghan. Canadian Newswire, "Canadians aren't risk-takers, but they are taking risks." Last modified 11/24/10. Accessed 01/05/12. http://www.newswire.calen/story/704549/canadians-aren-t-risk-takers-but-they-are-taking-risks.

If you have dependants and debt that would leave a burden on your family, you need to do the responsible thing and protect them with a good life insurance plan.

Why insurance makes sense

The pain and embarrassment of not being able to pay for the burial of my brother and my uncle made me question what my family was doing with their money. After a little digging, I came to realize that not one person in my family had ever taken out a policy to protect their loved ones. How could this be, since at some level they had to be aware of the importance of leaving something for them?

No one could say they didn't know about life insurance either, because television commercials reminded us daily. So what prevented my sister, uncles, and aunts from protecting their families, especially considering they all had young children living at home?

Didn't they get the message that life insurance was not for them but for the protection of their loved ones? I would go so far as to say life insurance is the most selfless thing you can do for your family, because you will never personally benefit from it.

Here is how I see it. When my brother passed, he left nothing for his family because he hadn't built a financial foundation. In fact, the topic of money and finance had never crossed his mind. I have learned priceless lessons from his life and made sure that all my affairs are in order so that my family will be in a position to survive financially without me.

Most people don't like to talk about death, and will put off indefinitely applying for life insurance or writing their wills. But I am sure you actually don't want those you care about to suffer because of your irresponsibility. Tackle the issue head on, and put together an appropriate plan to ensure your family is protected.

Who Needs It?

So does everyone need a $500,000-thousand-dollar policy, or is life insurance only for those who are old? I used to hear that question a lot. Many young people feel they are invincible, and that taking out a policy in their early 20s is a waste of their money.

Nothing could be further from the truth. Life insurance has more to do with the number of dependants and liabilities you have and less to do with your age. A man in his early 20s might be in need of more insurance than another in his early 40s. The younger man might be newly married with a child and a mortgage and monthly car payments. He might be the only income earner in his family, which means that if he died his family would suffer tremendous hardship. He clearly has dependants and liabilities that need to be insured.

Conversely, the man in his 40s might be single with no children and rent an apartment, be debt free, with enough money in his bank account to cover his final expenses. Clearly such a person is in a position much different from that of our 20-something, and doesn't need insurance. He might certainly have a policy if he wished to take one out, but his passing will not mean undue financial hardship for others.

When deciding if you need insurance, you should consider the two questions below. If you answer yes to one or both, you probably need to consider protecting your family by taking out a policy.

1. Is there a lot of outstanding debt that would leave your family members overwhelmed financially and possibly homeless because they do not have the resources to make future payments? These debts might be things like school loans, credit card payments, car payments, and outstanding mortgages.
2. Are there dependent children or other family members like older parents who rely on your income? How long would it take to replace that income, and will your family be in trouble without it?

These two factors should guide your insurance decision. This is not to say that you can't take it out anyway. Many people find it important to provide a little something for their loved ones, even if they are debt-free and without dependants. They see insurance as a way of leaving a small nest egg.

Regardless of what stage of life you are currently in, adequate protection for your family is a must.

What Type of Insurance Should You Buy?

It's amazing just how little is understood about life insurance by the general population. This is partly explained by the smooth sales agents who purposely confuse clients in an attempt to sell overpriced products that do not meet the client's needs.

The most oversold products are whole life policies, not because they offer superior protection for families but because they involve higher commissions to sales agents and more profits to the insurance companies. **[Whole life insurance provides permanent, lifetime protection for a level premium. Depending on the plan you buy, whole life insurance spreads the cost of your coverage over the lifetime of the policy or over a limited period of time].** It is important to note that the premiums for this kind of coverage will be higher than what you would pay for term insurance, sometimes almost as much as five times the monthly cost.

Many people flock to this kind of policy because it offers a cash-value that will accumulate over the years. **[The amount of money available in cash upon death or cancellation of the insurance policy by the owner, also called a cash surrender value].** This money grows tax-free, and should you cancel your insurance policy you will be able to get the money that has accrued in the cash value portion of your policy. Here is my question though: Why would you want to pay exorbitantly high premiums to fund a cash value account that gives you returns that are consistent with what you would get with a GIC or money market account? In my opinion it is not worth throwing your money away on such a policy.

If you already have an insurance policy, I encourage you to take a closer look at it. There is a good chance you have been sold a whole life or, worse, a universal life policy.

Universal life insurance should be avoided by the majority of Canadians, because this kind of coverage is a mystery to most people, including many brokers who sell it. The profile of an individual considering this type of policy should be as follows. He or she

1. Should have a need for life insurance;
2. Should be in a high marginal tax bracket;
3. Should want to create additional future income;
4. Should have already maximized RRSP and pension contributions;
5. May be paying too much tax on investment income; and
6. Should have an investment horizon of at least ten years.

If you don't fit this profile, you should not give in to the slick sales agent who tells you it provides the greatest flexibility and gives you control over how your money is invested. The universal life policy was not designed for the average income earner, so heed my advice and stay clear!

Now, there is nothing *inherently* wrong with either whole life or universal life insurance, but they are not right for the majority of people.

Your alternative is to purchase *term* insurance, which provides the greatest coverage depending on your age at the lowest cost. So what is the difference between term and whole life insurance?

To put it simply, whole (or permanent) life insurance provides financial protection for as long as someone lives and is paying the premiums. Term policies provide insurance coverage for a specific period, frequently 5, 10 or 20 years.

Buy Term Insurance and Invest the Difference

Term insurance is the most cost-effective in the marketplace, as it provides pure protection for you and your family without all the bells and whistles. [**Term life insurance provides coverage at a fixed price for a limited period of time, the relevant term. When that period expires, coverage ends and the client must either forgo coverage or renew with different payments or conditions**]. Depending on your age and health, a term life insurance policy will provide your family with the most coverage at lowest cost. You can now get a policy for as few as 5 years or as many as 35 years with some companies. Regardless of the liabilities you owe, 35 years should be more than enough time to pay them off and build your future wealth, especially if you follow the advice in this book. Most experts will tell you that term insurance is right for more than 90% of the population. With those percentages it is probably right for you as well.

Don't be swayed into buying insurance that promises to invest part of your premium payments. The promise of 2% or 3% return on the invested money should be enough to alert you that this is not a good idea. Insurance was created for protection, not as an investment vehicle. You will do much better buying term insurance and investing the money saved into one of the three vehicles for wealth creation that I will share with you later.

One more thing: the life insurance you get from your employer is not enough to protect your family should you die. On average, you need coverage of six to eight times your annual salary for those who survive you. The other thing to remember is that your life will be going through some major changes once your finances get back on track. This could mean that you might require additional coverage as your wealth grows, or maybe you will need to reduce your coverage. In either case you need to understand that your income protection ought to be designed to give you flexibility as you move through your life.

Mortgage insurance: Yes or No?

Millions of people refuse to take out personal life insurance, but opt into buying the *mortgage insurance* offered to them by the big banks. Before you go signing on the dotted line, there are some things you need to know about this product. First and foremost, I want to make it crystal-clear that it is not a wise investment.

Mortgage insurance is meant to cover the full cost of the outstanding mortgage should you die. It is offered to everyone who purchases a home regardless if the home is an investment or for personal residence. The rationale is that such a policy provides security and peace of mind for the homeowner. Many people feel they have to take out this insurance to protect their families, and of course the banks pressure them to buy it — especially if they are first-time homeowners with little knowledge about insurance.

For many people the purchase of a home is the biggest financial decisions of their lives. It conjures up strong emotions about whether one is doing the right thing in purchasing a particular home and if one can afford it. The banks play on these emotions, and are quick to add fear into the mix.

Here is what you should know. Mortgage insurance is a decreasing term insurance. This means that as you reduce the amount of your mortgage owed to the bank, the face amount of your death benefit is reduced to the amount of the mortgage outstanding. If you purchased mortgage insurance for $250,000 and have paid your mortgage down to $50,000 that is all the banks would pay your family upon your death. Mortgage insurance benefits the bank and ensures that your outstanding mortgage is paid in full should you pass away. It insures the bank, not you. This is a sad truth that you must know.

It hardly seems logical that the premiums you pay every month stay the same while the face amount of your death benefit decreases. An additional problem with these policies is that they have what is called "post-claim underwriting" this means that they don't decide if you are actually eligible for the insurance until after you die, after they have accepted your money for years and years. This can lead to huge legal battles with the insurance company. It also adds insult to injury for the surviving members of your family who are trying to bury their loved one and bring closure to the matter. *This is not a good insurance — never was, never will be!* Mortgage insurance is designed to protect only the banks, not the consumer.

Give your family peace of mind

My suggestion is to purchase term life insurance that is at least equal to the amount of your mortgage; it is the most cost-effective way and provides the largest benefit to your family. A 35-to-40-year term should be more than enough time to pay off your mortgage and build a solid financial nest-egg for your family. If it isn't, maybe you have bitten off far more than you can chew.

The advantage to term life is that *you pay the same premium for the life of your policy and the full face amount is paid to your family if you die.* If you purchased $350,000 of coverage and only have $50,000 outstanding on your mortgage when you die, your family gets the full $350,000. Your loved ones can pay the bank the $50,000 owed and get to keep the remaining $300,000. With term insurance you prove you are insurable *before* the policy is approved, meaning no legal fights with the insurance company later.

If you have just bought a home, you need to protect your family should you die. But make sure it is with the right kind of insurance … *TERM.* If you have already purchased mortgage insurance from your bank, I suggest you hurry and get it changed to personal life insurance.

Keep your guard up

Nancy's Story

It was the summer of 2007 when I first met Nancy. I had just finished one of my Friday-night training sessions at the YMCA and was on my way home when a car driven by a bubbly young woman pulled up beside mine.

We had a very brief conversation about what we each did for a living and why we were both passionate about physical fitness. In her mid-20s, she was a psychologist who loved her job. I shared that I was a middle-school vice-principal and a "financial fitness trainer" (at that time an insurance representative). It was late in the evening, but we felt comfortable exchanging numbers and promised to be in touch to learn more about each other in the near future.

We called each other a few times after our first meeting and found we had a lot in common. Unfortunately, life happens, and we lost contact for about a year before reconnecting. I had recently returned from a real estate trip to Thunder Bay and decided to give her a call to see how she was doing.

She was glad to hear from me, and asked if I was still in the field of finance. I told her I was, and that a big part of what I was now doing was teaching others about the merits of investing in real estate. She asked if I would have any time in my schedule to meet up for a conversation. I could tell from the sound of her voice that she clearly had something she wanted to discuss. I told her I would be more than happy to meet with her to see how I could be of service.

We had lunch to talk about her situation and what she wanted for herself. Nancy startled me when she revealed that for the past three years she had been paying $500.00 a month into an insurance policy sold to her by a family friend. She was 26 years old. Can you say ouch? As they say, with friends like that you don't need enemies.

She had been sold, not one, but two, universal life policies, a product usually reserved for sophisticated or accredited investors. Universal life has its place in the life insurance market, but to sell it to a 23-year-old just starting her career is downright sinful. The only thing this agent cared about was the big commission cheques she would be earning. But this is what happens when you don't understand things or take the time to become financially literate. I am not blaming Nancy; she was supposedly being advised by a family friend and didn't know she needed to have her guard up. But I was surprised that her family was not able to talk her out of it (not that they didn't try).

So I made another appointment to visit her and take a closer look at the policy she had been sold. I remember asking her how the heck she had gotten herself into this position. She had an insurance policy that covered her for one million dollars, but had no dependants and didn't even own a home. Our conversation went something like this:

"Why are you paying a $500.00 premium for a $1,000,000 policy when you clearly don't need insurance right now?"

"Well, this is what I was told to do by the agent who sold me the policies. I knew something was wrong and recently cancelled one of the policies but I am still paying $250.00 every month for the one policy."

"What do your parents think about all this?"

"Well, they think it's stupid."

"So you didn't listen to them?"

"No, I didn't."

"So why are you coming to me with this?"

"Well, I have had a chance to speak with you and I know you are helping others with this stuff, so I thought I should just talk to you so I can get your opinion."

I said, "Listen to your parents. What you are doing right now is throwing good money at a bad idea. The only ones benefiting from your $250.00 monthly payment are the agent and the company who sold you the policy. You need to get rid of it as soon as possible."

I probed a little more. Nancy was in a hole for sure. She had outstanding student loans and credit card bills, and yet here she was virtually killing herself to pay a huge chunk of cash every month toward a policy she didn't need.

"So what can I do to fix the mess I am in?" she asked.

"If you are willing to trust me and follow my advice, we can put you on a much better path," I told her.

"I trust you, so let's get to work."

Like many women, Nancy loved shopping and spared no expense to have the best when it came to clothing and her shoes. I spoke to her about the importance of curtailing that nasty habit if she was going to take control of her financial future. She agreed that she would make the needed changes.

Although Nancy had no immediate need for insurance, she wanted to buy a home within the next two years. Despite her financial situation, this was well within her reach because she was already earning an income in the mid-six-figures. We decided that a 35-year-term policy with a face amount of $300,000 would be more than enough for her immediate needs. We could always revisit that coverage as her personal situation changed. By changing her policy to term insurance, Nancy was able to free up more than $200.00 a month. That money was then directed toward paying off her high-interest credit card and student loans.

The investment segment of her universal life policy was transferred to a segregated fund that paid a higher rate of interest than the 2% to 3% she was earning in the other policy. Nancy was excited by these changes, and was able to see a light at the end of the tunnel.

Nancy called me six months later to tell me she was ready to buy her first home. She said it was going to cost $400,000. I expressed my disapproval and told her I didn't think she was in a position to take on that much additional debt. She wasn't out of the woods yet debt-wise, and besides she should really have been considering a cheaper condo for her first purchase. In the end, reason prevailed and she walked away from the idea of becoming a homeowner just then.

A year later it was a different story. Nancy had read some of the books I had recommended to increase her financial literacy, and had followed the simple disciplines explained in order to pay off her debts. She was now ready to buy a home, and had found the perfect place. She asked how much of her RRSP could be used for her down payment and was told up to $20,000 for first-time home buyers. So we went ahead and got the money transferred to her account.

I asked her what she was doing about mortgage rates. She told me she had gone to the bank and they had given her a good rate. Hold the phone, I told her. Don't sign anything until I get back to you. What might look like a good rate is more than likely not in your best interest. I gave Nancy the name and phone number of one of the brokers I use for my real estate purchases, and within a few hours Nancy had secured an interest rate 0.5 basis points better than what she would have gotten with the bank.

As a financial fitness trainer, my goal when working with a client is to show them the bigger picture, to help them realize what is available so they can proceed in a rational manner. Nancy is now on the right track, and has made significant advances toward her financial fitness goals. She has a bright financial future ahead of her, and with the income she now commands and increases to come in the future, she should be able to chart a course to financial freedom without difficulty. She now understands that "cash flow is king" and has shown some interest in the area of real estate investing as a vehicle for creating wealth for her future. Most importantly, she has raised her awareness of what is possible and now keeps her guard up when making decisions that involve her hard-earned dollars.

Chapter Seven

Financial Fitness

As we move into this most important of chapters I want you to reflect on the questions I am about to ask. They were posed by the late Jim Rohn on one of his CD series[19] I listened to religiously during my many drives from Toronto to Sault Ste. Marie, Cornwall, and Windsor.

These questions forced me to reflect on my life and assess if I was happy with all I had become. More importantly, it made me pause to consider the untapped possibilities available to me if only I woke from my slumber and put together a workable plan to achieving my dreams. I put these two questions to you in the hope that you will give them more than a cursory glance before moving on.

The first question is: If we could do better, should we?

The second is: If we agree that we should do better, will we?

One of the biggest issues of life is whether each of us is truly tapping into our full potential. Could we earn more or do more? Could we plan better or talk better? Could we give more or learn more to become more?

Most of you would reply that we certainly could. But the sad truth is that all of us *could,* most of us *should,* some of us *intend to,* but few of us *do.* That is the story of human progress, and I must tell you that for 35 years I followed the lead of the masses, content with my meager earnings

---

19   Rohn, Jim. Nightingale Conant, "Cultivating Your Enterprising Nature." http://www.nightingale.com/AE_Article-i-282-article-CultivatingEnterprisingNature.aspx.

and lack of progress. I definitely knew I should and could do better, but didn't take the necessary steps.

Luckily my long drives to Sault Ste. Marie listening to hours of thought-provoking audio showed me the light. Once that light was turned on, I vowed never to stand still and be swept away by indecision and resignation.

This book is about financial fitness. It is about creating your life by taking charge of your money so you can leave a legacy for generations to come. Many of you know you could do better, and should do better with the gifts you have been given. My question is: Will you?

When all is said and done, the fruits of your labour will be the measuring stick of your success. Make sure you take full responsibility for the results you achieve. Those results will be based on your efforts and nothing else.

You will need to stay hungry. Hungry people are willing to do today the things others won't do, to have tomorrow the things others won't have. They are willing to pay whatever price is necessary in advance. They invest in themselves by attending seminars and workshops. They are always searching, always seeking higher ground so they can grow to their full potential.

Remember, you don't get in life what you want; you get in life what you are. To build a better you, you must program yourself for success by surrounding yourself with people who are doing the things you want to do. Success leaves clues, so you want to learn as much as you can from the examples of others.

To stay hungry is the key ingredient that will keep you coming back again and again when life's obstacles appear. People that are hungry are unstoppable. They will get things done no matter what. How hungry are you? Are you hungry enough to do all that is required for the achievement of your financial dreams?

Why you must become financially fit

I cannot tell you the number of sleepless nights I spent worrying about money early in my career. I would lie awake trying to calculate how much was needed to pay my bills and how much if any would be left at the end of the month. Here I was in the early years of my teaching career, earning a higher income than the average Canadian, yet I could hardly keep up. I couldn't help wondering how those making less than I was could manage the daily financial hurdles of life.

Maybe I could have made things a bit more manageable for myself by stretching out the payments on my student loans, but I absolutely hated the thought of owing money. I wanted no one to have a claim on me, so I decided to pay off my student loans in three years and that is exactly what I did.

That was definitely not a fun period. I had to make many sacrifices to ensure I didn't get myself into greater financial trouble. I restricted myself to buying only what was absolutely necessary. I couldn't afford to get caught up in our consumer-driven society or hang out at the bars foolishly spending money to impress people who would never recognize me if they passed me on the street. My focus was on getting out of debt quickly, and I was starting to develop a hunger for the other side of the balance sheet.

Jim Rohn once defined financial fitness as "the ability to live off the resources of your own personal creation." Wow! Isn't that what we all want? To be in a position where no one has a claim on us, where money is no longer an obstacle, and we are free to do as we want, when we want, with whom we want? Only a few will ever achieve this elusive ideal. Will you be one of them? Or will you settle and fall back in with the crowd out of fear of the work needed?

Take a good look around you. Do you see wealth and abundance around every corner? Wealth is everywhere. It is displayed in the homes people buy, the cars they drive, and the lives they live. And it is within the grasp of anyone willing to follow the principles discussed here, with total and unwavering commitment.

If you don't see wealth, then what do you see? Are you looking at the world through a poverty lens and listening to the doom and gloom of our media outlets? When you hear the news that Europe's financial system will soon implode, do you throw up your hands and surrender to a life of mediocrity, or do you say this is one more reason to create financial freedom in my life? As discussed earlier, your outer world is merely a reflection of your inner attitude. Change the attitude on the inside and your outer world will also change.

Creating wealth is not your "destiny." It is a personal choice, and only you can decide whether it is important for you. But if you truly want to become all you can possibly be, I would strongly suggest you commit yourself to the dream — call it economic success, financial fitness, getting rich, or whatever you wish.

As I mentioned at the beginning of this book, my early upbringing involved much sitting in church listening to scriptures that "The love of money is the root of all evil" and "It is easier for a camel to pass through the eye of a needle than for a rich man to enter the kingdom of heaven." It is easy to see how messages like these can cloud our reality, and why so many adults have great difficulty finding financial security let alone financial freedom.

Fortunately for me, the veil was lifted from my eyes several years ago. First of all, as was discussed earlier, the *love of money* is not the same thing as *money itself.* Secondly, money itself is not the root of all evil ... *poverty* is. Poverty will rob you of ambition and leads to all manner of evil deeds. Being consistently broke the day before payday is evil; it leads to lies, dishonesty, and the loss of dignity and self-esteem. The lack of money to meet one's basic needs is often behind theft, divorce, and family discontent. Yes, the lack of money is evil, as it erodes the moral fabric of life.

The absence of money is merely an effect. *We* are the cause. A lot of people want an above-average job with above-average pay, but they are not willing to do above-average work or become an above-average person. They believe all they have to do is make positive affirmations on a daily basis, and the universe will reward them. This is rubbish. The only way to attract more abundance in your life is to increase your value by becoming more.

You must read good books. They showcase a wealth of collected experiences, both of those who have failed but since succeeded, and of those who have succeeded but since failed. Mulling over ideas from those in a position to know is one of the best ways to accelerate your progress.

Opportunities are all around you; take a look, and commit yourself to either getting serious or getting out. Do not linger in unproductivity, uncertainty, or mediocrity — you were born for greatness.

Begin an all-out pursuit. Get there as quickly as possible so that never again do you have to check menu prices before you enter a restaurant, or fear a ringing phone or the sight of monthly bills in the mail. You want money out of the way as a consideration for the process of life.

Money is not everything, and it won't buy you happiness, but it is better to have it in abundance than to be without it. Money is in itself neither good nor bad. It is merely a magnifier; it makes you more of who you already are. If you are a thoughtful person who gives to charity, you will do more for others when your finances are in order. If you are a mean person who only does for himself, money will only make you meaner and more obnoxious.

You want money so you can live a rich and rewarding life. You want money because with it and with the strategies for how to create it, you can pass that knowledge on to others. Money is the key, but in order to attract it into your life you must have crystal-clear goals for its attainment.

Goals

If you are to achieve any notable level of success in your financial future, you must begin with a solid plan. Otherwise you are kidding yourself. Your goals provide the roadmap by which you will travel to the destinations you have set at predetermined points in the future.

Without goals your future is left to chance and your odds of success are markedly reduced. It is like an archer shooting at a target 100 yards away at night. It doesn't matter how accomplished the archer is, the probability of hitting the target is close to zero. But put that archer in a well-lit environment where he or she can clearly see the target and the chance of success increases dramatically. Clear goals provide direction and focus for your life and will keep you on track when the rough weather sets in.

Setting Goals

Many of you have probably seen the acronym "SMART" hundreds of times, and some of you might have even committed the specific words to your memory. It is often used in workshops to illustrate the specific components of effective goal-setting. I believe it is worth speaking of its importance at this point.

As an educator I know much time is spent teaching this acronym to students from the primary grades all the way through university and grad school. Why? Because it works, and "If it ain't broke, don't fix it."

SMART means your goals must be **S**pecific, **M**easurable, **A**chievable, **R**ealistic, and **T**ime-based for you to be successful. These five key points by themselves will not help you set SMART goals, so I will explain each in detail before moving on.

For your goals to be **specific** there can be no vagueness about what you want to accomplish with your finance, your health, your career, your relationships, etc. You must clearly define what it is you want to accomplish. "I want to be rich" is too general. What do you mean by rich? Everyone has a different idea of what that means. Does it mean accumulating $500,000 in your investment account, or does it mean having a $1,000,000 net worth? You must write down exactly what it is you want to accomplish.

When I was getting ready for my third-degree black belt grading a few years ago, I weighed approximately 184 pounds. Now, I wasn't overweight by any stretch of the imagination. I just wanted to lose a few pounds so

I would be in optimum condition for the demands of my grading. But I didn't express it like that to myself. What I wrote down was that I wanted to lose eight to ten pounds by the time of my grading. Then I went to work, and a few months later I had successfully completed my grading weighing 173 pounds.

The second component of your SMART goal is that it must be **measurable**. You can't have clearly defined goals without benchmarks to measure your progress. If your goal is to increase your passive income by $1,500 per year, how will you know you are on the right track? What yardstick will you use? Maybe, for you, that means purchasing three properties that yield an average return of $500.00 per month.

Maybe your goals aren't related to financial matters. When I was getting ready for my grading and had the goal of losing ten pounds, my yardstick was to see a two-pound decrease every week leading up to the grading. That kept me on track, with my goals at the forefront of my mind.

The third component is that your goal must be **achievable**. This does not mean that you should do what most people do, which is to set goals that don't allow them to stretch or get out of their comfort zone. Don't join this group of low achievers. But also, don't shoot for the moon.

The key is to shoot for a target a little nearer than the moon when you first begin setting goals. For example, if you have never invested in the stock market, it would be very unwise to set a goal for a 15% or 20% return. Shooting for the big returns is probably unachievable and will leave you in a world of hurt when the other shoe falls. It is more reasonable to expect 4-8 percent rate of return on your money while protecting your principal from loss.

The fourth component of your SMART goal is to set **realistic** expectations. Many people want instant success and lack the patience to stick with a plan or nurture the seeds they have planted until it bears fruit. They have little or no awareness of what's required to move them from one rung of the financial success ladder to the next.

If you have never bought an investment property, don't set goals to have three 20-unit commercial buildings in your first year. This is out of reach for even the most seasoned investor.

Wealth creation is a process that requires you to grow from the inside as well as the outside. Remember, what you are on the inside determines what you will manifest on the outside. Your success will be based on a sound philosophy grounded in adopting the simple disciplines of life.

So instead of shooting for three commercial buildings, you might make it your goal to buy one multi-family investment property, or a smaller commercial building, so you don't get taken to the cleaners.

The final component of the SMART goal is that it must be **time-based**. Having a deadline forces you to get off your butt and put the pedal to the metal. It allows you to work backward and define checkpoints along the way to ensure you stay on track for success.

I cannot overemphasize how vitally important this last component is. Without a deadline, there is no urgency to achieve great things, no accountability. Instead you just meander through life playing the victim and blaming others for your lack of accomplishment. With it, you take charge of your destiny and hold yourself accountable for your actions and the results you attain.

I would hazard a guess that if you are reading this book, you have most likely heard about the power of goal-setting. Why, then, do so few people use the strategies highlighted above? Could it be that they are already at the apex of their financial journey and personal development? I highly doubt it.

Could it be that the initial work required to overcome decades of inertia is just too overwhelming for most? Remember, you will have to pay the price either up front or in the end. I am telling you it is far easier to pay the price when you are young and healthy than when the years have robbed you of your youth and vitality.

If you are still in your 30s and 40s, you still have time on your side. Let others continue to live small lives if they so choose. Your life can be created to order, and all you need to do is to decide what you truly want, put your SMART plan together, and get to work.

Chapter Eight

Personal Development

You can't build your future unless you know your past. So let's take a close look at the facts. If you are reading this book you are probably between the ages of 25 and 50. Some of you are making six-figure incomes but most of you have incomes that are barely meeting your increasing expenses. You are concerned about the economic uncertainty in the media and the doom-and-gloom forecasts of economists. What can you do?

One option is to give up on your retirement dreams of comfort and security and accept a future of an increasingly meager existence, growing bitter and blaming the government and the powers that be for the mess you are in.

Another thought might be: Enough is enough already! I'm not getting any younger, so I'd better change course and take full responsibility for where I am and where I want to end up. It's time to take the advice I've received and follow the lead of successful people so I can build a solid financial future.

You have options when it comes to how you want to live your life. You can blame others, or take responsibility. Blame will get you nowhere, but responsibility will get you to take action. Life was not meant to be easy. The twists and turns along with the ups and downs of life are what allow us to grow and develop. Life happens to all of us, and many of the events are often beyond our control. Some things will knock the wind out of us and make us question the merits of moving forward. You can't control the blows of life that come one way or another, but you have full and utter control in how you decide to respond to them.

When you are halfway through your life and barely making ends meet, it seems like the only chance to become financially fit is to play the lottery or go gambling. But your odds of becoming a millionaire by going after your dreams with dogged determination are far greater than those of winning the lottery or finding lady luck at the casino.

Those who have achieved financial success did not do so by playing the odds. They had goals for a better future, put a solid game plan together, and got to work. You can do the same. If you are not where you want to be financially, with the right attitude, passion for learning, and dedication you can become financially independent in five to ten years, fifteen tops. It is simple to do but it is not easy. However, if you are willing to do the work required it is definitely possible.

For the first 35 years of my life I was operating on the wrong plan, and I didn't know any other way. It took years of hard work and personal development to reshape my thinking and change my outlook in order to override the errors in my outlook and open up a new world of possibilities.

If I can do it, so can you. The first thing you will need to do is to accept the fact that you are solely and completely responsible for your current financial situation. There isn't likely going to be any knight in shining armour coming to your rescue with a fat inheritance.

By assuming responsibility for your current condition, you also take charge of your future. The sooner you accept that reality, the sooner you will shed the anger and blame and begin to feel financially powerful.

I'm telling you the truth, because I have done it myself and have coached others to do the same. It is a simple adjustment of your thinking, but it is extremely powerful. It works instantaneously. Without it, you cannot move forward.

Much of what is needed has already been provided in the earlier chapters of this book. But now I wish to share some specific strategies that have allowed millions to achieve financial success regardless of their meager beginnings. The key to better days is now being passed to you. All you have to do is put it in the lock, turn the handle, and walk into your bright financial future.

But first you will need the following three steps to unleash your greatness:

1. **Work harder on yourself than you do on the job.** This will be critically important, as it is the key to increasing your income. It is true that, regardless of where you begin, you can achieve financial success. But let us be brutally honest. The man who earns a six-figure income and practises the simple disciplines is in a far better position to achieve his financial dreams than the one who makes minimum wage. Nevertheless, the latter can enable his climb to the top by self-improvement that increases his ability to earn.

2. **Make your home a profitable investment.** I am constantly amazed by the number of people who are house-rich but cash-poor. They have the most beautiful homes money can buy, but are one or two paycheques away from financial ruin. Their pride and ignorance got them to bite off more than they can chew, and instead of learning what is needed to make their investment more profitable they are more concerned with appearances and continue to throw good money into the wind.

3. **Understand that profits are better than wages,** and you will need to drive one of three profit vehicles across the financial fitness finish line. Those vehicles are *stocks, business ownership, and real estate.* You can choose to drive just one of these or any combination of them. The choice is up to you, each of them has its pros and cons. But regardless of which you choose, be sure you drive *through* the finish line, not to the finish line. When it comes to your financial future, this is one race you absolutely must win. Coming up short in this area will leave you with lifelong regrets.

The good news is that the strategies outlined in this book are time-tested and will get you the results you want. You can take comfort in knowing that your past is just that, your past. Where you were and where you are presently is not the sum total of where you will end up. Let's begin. For the rest of this chapter I will cover the first two steps. The third will follow in a chapter of its own.

Increase Your Ability to Earn

If you are in your middle years, 35 and older, you already know the hands of time are moving fast and ticking loudly. So what can you do when you are running short on time? You must increase your ability to earn.

The quickest way to do this is to "Work harder on yourself than you do on your job." I must admit when I first heard this I didn't really understand what it meant. But as I continued with my studies and followed the teachings of some of the best in the field of personal development I started to get it. It is said if you work hard on your job you can make a living, but if you work hard on yourself you can make a fortune. So how will this increase your ability to earn?

Working harder on yourself means to focus your attention on your own personal development. Take stock of your daily errors in judgment and their true cost to your financial future. How much time is wasted watching television and other non-productive activities? Why not turn over a new leaf and devote that time to wealth-building instead? Here's a novel idea — read! All the answers to the questions of life have already been recorded.

You must read books, listen to CDs, and attend the seminars that will open your mind to the unlimited potential within. The books you don't read cannot help you, but the ones you do read can unlock the doors to your future wealth. Can you devote 30 minutes a day to reading? Of course you can, it is easy to do; but, guess what? It is also easy not to do. Thirty minutes or ten pages a day is 3,550 pages for the year. That is the equivalent of 10–15 thought-provoking books that can have a dramatic effect on how your life plays out.

I hear some of you saying you don't have the time to read. Well, then, you must be willing to accept the fact that your current circumstances will not likely change.

Over the years I have become a serious seeker of learning, reading at every opportunity. I have turned my car into a drive-time university so I can listen to the teachings and the philosophy of successful people. I read while working on my cardio at the gym — why not work on my physical and mental fitness at the same time? It saves me time and produces results physically and mentally. Still don't have time to read? Do what I did, buy a CD and turn off your radio.

Just 30 minutes a day and your life will never be the same. So go ahead, I give you permission: cast aside the comfortable shoes of victimization and take control.

Working harder on yourself means making the hard decisions to limit your association with negative people. These people have the ability to suck all the energy out of a room and they will bring you down with them. We all know that misery loves company, and negative people are always looking for recruits to support their cause. So do whatever is necessary to increase your time associating with successful people who see opportunity when others see obstacles, so you can learn from them.

Working harder on yourself means going beyond what is asked of you and providing more service than you get paid to do. This strategy alone will yield a favourable return.

About three years ago, I was the vice-principal of a Middle School in southeast Scarborough. One of my responsibilities was to book competent supply teachers for our building when our regular teachers were absent. This was not always an easy task, as the strength of the supply pool was very limited.

Many teachers would work for the day, say thanks, and be on their way. A few would drop by my office and ask point-blank if there was anything I could do to get them a permanent job. Times were tough when it came to landing a job with the Toronto District School Board, and they still are, but a better question would have been: "What can I do to secure a job with the board?"

One teacher, stood out from the rest in her approach to teaching and learning. She would be at the school early and often stayed later than the others to mark papers or leave notes for the classroom teacher.

One evening I saw her in one of the classrooms working on long-range plans. Curious, I asked her why she was working on those when she didn't have a class of her own. "I just want to learn how to do them for when I get my own class" was her response. I quickly filed her answer in my memory.

A few weeks later I was holding an audition for our first *Brant Idol* (our own version of *American Idol* to showcase our students' musical skills) and none of my teaching staff could find the time to volunteer and help me out. Along came the supply teacher. Not only did she stay and help me until after 5 p.m., but she made sure she attended the night of the performance and even paid admission. Wow!

She definitely went above and beyond, providing far more service than she was being paid for. A few days after our Brant Idol competition, I got an email from another administrator looking for a strong teacher to fill a long-term position. Guess who I recommended? Today Hellen is a full-time teacher with the board, still going above and beyond to hone her skills and provide the best for her students.

By working harder on yourself, developing a pleasing personality and a positive mental attitude, you will become an attractive person. Your ability to engage and draw people to you is a powerful asset in the workplace, and will not go unnoticed. By doing these seemingly simple things you will immediately separate yourself from others in your company. You will become what I like to call the "purple snowflake," a person whom employers notice. Employers are looking for leaders who get results, work well with others, and can inspire others.

Working harder on yourself will make you invaluable to your employer. **When you are invaluable you create employment security in a non job security world.**

Turn Your House into a Cash Machine

Robert Kiyosaki, author of *Rich Dad, Poor Dad* among others, has spoken of the importance of *leverage* in building lasting wealth. He goes on to use the acronym OPM (other people's money) throughout many of his books in order to highlight for the reader the incredible power of leveraging at work.

So what is leverage, and how can it help you build lasting wealth and eliminate debt (especially your mortgage)? Although there are many forms of it, I will be referring to *financial leverage* in my example. [**For our purpose leverage is the use of various financial instruments or borrowed capital, like margin, to increase the potential return of an investment**].

In this context, leverage is the degree to which an investor or business utilizes borrowed money. When done properly, financial leverage can increase one's return on investments or markedly reduce one's overall debt. A word of caution: individuals who are too highly leveraged may be at risk of financial disaster (bankruptcy) if they are unable to make payments on their debt. This could have dramatic effects on your credit score and limit your ability to acquire funds from lenders in the future.

Several years ago I got smart to the idea of using leverage to eliminate high-interest credit card debts. I had several credit cards, but carried a balance on only one of them. I contacted the card companies that I did not have a balance with and asked if they had any promotional rates coming up. Many responded favourably and offered rates as low as 0.9% or 1.9% for six to nine months on balance transfers. This was great news for me. I was able to transfer my high-interest balance to the low-interest cards, saving hundreds in interest payments. As the promotional periods came to an end, I again made calls to see who was offering a promotional rate and transferred my balance to those cards. In effect, I was now an investor using the system to help eliminate interest payments and keep money in my pocket.

How does this apply to your mortgage? Well, imagine that you are carrying a $400,000-dollar mortgage at 3.5% fixed interest for five years, amortized over 35 years. It is the home of your dreams, and you can't see yourself living anywhere else. You can afford the payments and still have a little bit left over at the end of the month to put toward your investment plan. But you are a little disheartened by the fact that you will be paying a mortgage until you are in your mid-60s.

What can you do? Do what I did, and leverage the bank's money to pay off that mortgage in one-half to one-third of the time. Here are the facts:

Cost of a $400,000 home at 3.5% interest	**$1,647.32 per month**
Interest paid for the 5-year term	**$66,842.06**
Interest paid on 35 year amortization	**$291,870.90**
Principal owed after 5 years	**$368,002.86**
Amount owed after 18 years of payment	**$253,495.05**

How is your dream home looking now? It will cost you a total of $691,870.90 to live in your home unless you decide to do something different.

I understand that the banks need to get paid for putting up the majority of the money for our homes. In some cases they will put up 95% of the value of the house just so you can call it your own. I also understand that the banks are in business to make money, and I have absolutely no problem with that. If you are in business and you are not making a profit maybe you should get out of it and find something else to do. However, I do have a problem with the outrageous amounts of unnecessary interest homeowners pay to provide basic shelter for our families.

Did you notice what I said just now? I said I am **outraged by the unnecessary** amount of **interest we pay** to carry our mortgages. If something is unnecessary, it means we have a choice in whether we do it or not. If I have lost you please replace the word "unnecessary" with "avoidable." Yes, you and I, and millions of others, continue to pay avoidable interest to the banks to the tune of hundreds of thousands over the life of our mortgages, because we are unaware of the options we have to eliminate this debt in short order.

So what can you do? Before getting into the short version of what I do, let's start with some basics. First, you must understand that the banks (most of them) have given you some flexibility for paying off your mortgage and reducing your borrowing cost. They know that not everyone out there is financially illiterate and wish to stay in perpetual servitude to them. However, they are banking on the fact that the majority lack the savvy to take advantage of these flexible options provided to reduce their mortgage debt.

Most banks will allow you to pay your mortgage, weekly, biweekly, or monthly. I pay biweekly, as this allows me to make one extra monthly mortgage payment every year. You will save a few dollars doing this (but don't expect to be dining on champagne and caviar).

You can also increase your monthly or biweekly payment by 20%. The great thing about this strategy is that the extra amount goes right against the principal and eliminates unnecessary interest in the future. If you have extra money at the end of the month, this could be a great way to eliminate your debt and increase your wealth at the same time.

Some banks will allow you to prepay 10%, 20% or even 25% on the anniversary date of your mortgage. This amount is applied directly to your outstanding principal. Few among us have the discipline or the financial resources to save 20% or 25% of our mortgage and pay it on the anniversary date. The banks that only use this method of prepayment are stacking your debt in their favour, so do your research before signing on the dotted line.

A better option is to make prepayments throughout the year up to a maximum of 20% or 25% of your mortgage. This is like gold, and if used correctly will help you reduce your borrowing cost and increase your wealth.

Here is an example of how the prepayment option works in your favour. If you have extra money at the end of the month, leverage the bank's money and attack your mortgage principal to eliminate your debt. Let's say you have read this entire book and have practised the disciplined habits I have outlined for you, so that you have reduced your expenses and hold $1,000 of discretionary income available every month. How does this impact your wealth? Take a look and be the judge.

You are still carrying the $400,000 mortgage at 3.5% fixed for 5 years and your monthly payments are the same	$1647.32
Monthly extra principal payment	$1000 for 5 years
Interest paid on 5-year term	$60,372.20
Total interest saved on mortgage	$102,000.00
Years saved	8.2
Balance owed after 5 years,	$301,533.00
Balance owed after 18 years	$149,138.53

These are the facts. Understanding how money works and how to effectively leverage other people's money is a sure way to financial success.

But what if you only have a few hundred available to you at the end of the month? Is there nothing you can do? If I had $500.00 at the end of the month, I might do the following. Borrow $4,000 from my line of credit and pay it directly toward my mortgage principal. Even at 5% interest it will only cost me $200.00 for the year or $16.67 a month to service the debt on the line of credit. Some of you might be questioning why on earth would you borrow from a higher interest account to pay against a lower interest mortgage? For starters each additional payment you make against your mortgage attacks the principal amount owed. This reduces the length of the amortization period on your loan and eliminates thousands in unnecessary interest payments. Secondly because your mortgage owed is in the hundreds of thousands, the annual interest you are paying is significantly higher than the simple interest charged on your lines of credit. When I take a look at the numbers between doing nothing, and leveraging my line of credit to pay down my mortgage, my decision is a no-brainer. Paying a few hundred dollars on my LOC to save tens of thousands off my mortgage interest is a price I will gladly pay any day of the week.

Let's continue with this example, every month I would pay $500.00 from my discretionary funds against my line of credit. In less than eight months my line of credit would be back to zero, and I would repeat the process and continue to attack my mortgage in that manner.

You don't have to pay unnecessary amounts of interest on your mortgage. You do have options. Just imagine the freedom and sense of accomplishment you would gain knowing that you have total control over your biggest financial debt. For many years I operated on the wrong philosophy, but once I understood that money gives you options and is merely a magnifier of the type of person you are, I started to turn my life around.

It would be irresponsible of me to move on before sharing one additional strategy for making your house a profitable investment.

When I bought my second home I didn't understand the power of money and how it truly worked. I was still putting in hours for dollars as a bouncer in a night club just to make ends meet. For seven years I had been struggling with the bills and working every weekend at a job I did not enjoy. I didn't know there was a virtual gold mine in my own house just waiting for me to dig and claim my share.

What was that gold mine you ask? It was two beautifully furnished rooms that stood empty for seven years that might have increased my income by at least $1,000 a month! Here I had been looking everywhere for additional sources of income but failed to look in my own back yard. That was a very costly lesson. ***Sometimes it is hard to see the whole picture when you are inside the frame.***

This strategy might not work for everyone, and some of you might feel uncomfortable taking in boarders. But if you are serious about achieving financial fitness and are running out of time, you might give it serious thought.

That extra room would provide a safe and affordable space for an ambitious and dedicated student. Many foreign students could use a supportive and nurturing environment while thousands of miles from their families and friends. Think about it — not only would you be helping them but you would be helping yourself in the process. You might even consider investing a few thousand to renovate your basement, and rent it out to a family trying to get their finances in order. The renovations if done correctly would increase your property value and some of the expenses would be tax deductible – awesome!

Some of you are sitting on gold mines that could alleviate much of the financial burden you are now faced with. All you have to do is pick up your shovel and start digging. All of us could, most of us should, some of us intend to, but few of us do.

Chapter Nine

Profits Are Better Than Wages

*Profits are better than wages. Wages will make you a living.
Profits can make you a fortune.*

—Jim Rohn

"Go to school, get a good education and find yourself a job that pays you well." Does this sound familiar to you, or am I the only one sold that message by my parents, teachers, and the rest of society? If you are reading this book, then it is highly probable you have been fed the same line growing up. Although this thinking might have yielded positive results several generations ago, it is no longer a sure thing when it comes to securing your financial future.

Gone are the days when an employee could expect to work for one company for forty years and retire with a defined-benefit pension plan. Today's employees have to continually upgrade themselves by taking courses to increase their knowledge and skills. They have to become lifelong learners with transferable skills or they might someday find themselves on the wrong end of the unemployment line.

Yes, times have changed, and it is now common for the average employee to work for four or five companies during his or her career. Unfortunately, the majority in this group (approximately 80%) still have the erroneous idea that their employer will take care of them and reward them for a lifetime of service.

They are badly mistaken, and have nothing but anger and resentment awaiting them unless they make some changes. You need to understand that no one is going to take care of you. Not your employer, not your government, not your parents, and certainly not your children. Your financial future is 100% your responsibility and only you can determine if it will be bright or gloomy.

Here is another sobering piece of news for you: if you are working a 9-to-5 job you are going to have to do more if you plan to finish ahead of the crowd and claim your financial freedom. I am not saying it is impossible to become financially free working 9-to-5, but the process can be quite slow unless you think ahead and do things outside the box. This means you will need to change your context and adopt a new philosophy and embrace the fact that profits are better than wages.

Wages will make you a living, but profits will make you a fortune. As an employee you get taxed at a higher level than those who are self-employed, business owners, or investors. You get no favourable tax breaks from your government and you are an expense to your employer. Your time is not your own. You are told when to report to work, when you can take a break, and for how long. And if you mess up too often you can expect to be shown the door.

You have absolutely no job security, and the current economic landscape with thousands of companies downsizing may have you on pins and needles wondering if your job could be next. Your time is sold to whatever employer is willing to pay you the most number of dollars for your hours, and you fear asking for a raise even though your expenses have increased dramatically.

If you are lucky, you get three weeks' vacation per year, but if you are sick outside of those dates you feel guilty asking for a day off. In short, you are a slave to the job, with one eye on the clock, waiting for the workday to end. Most likely you are getting paid just enough to keep you from quitting, and you are doing just enough to keep from getting fired. It is easy to see why financial freedom is so elusive for those who devote their working lives to a job.

I also work 9-to-5, and I love it. One of the greatest joys of this job is having former students return years later to tell you how your words had an impact on their lives.

While I am grateful for all I have, I am constantly in pursuit of more. For me this is why I believe profits are better than wages. Now please don't misunderstand me. I am not telling you to give up your day job and start your own business. What I am telling you is that you will need to find other strategies outside your 9-to-5 employment that will allow you to earn additional income and get your finances under control.

Profits have a way of changing your whole attitude, even if you start part-time — whether it's on your entrepreneurial business, network marketing company, or service business, it doesn't matter.

It might be training, consulting, or tutoring. It might be based on a hobby, like painting, writing, crafts, or computers. It might be something seasonal, like a landscape business in the summer or hanging Christmas lights in the winter. I have a friend who earns more decorating car dealerships, sport centres, and seniors' homes than from his regular job.

Think how empowering that would be, to go to work each and every day knowing you are working on your fortune. If you are willing to remain disciplined and continue the process, your part-time job might one day turn into your full-time passion.

I was never one to shy away from work, but as I got older and (hopefully) a little wiser, I realized that I had wasted far too much time trading hours for dollars. I no longer look for jobs that require additional hours to earn an income. Now I focus on opportunities where my money can be employed to do the heavy lifting and not me.

Romeo's Story

A few years ago I had the pleasure of teaching a six-week course to students at a Middle school. Twice a week for two hours, I presented "Financially Fit Teens." I taught students the value of saving part of all they earned, of giving to charity and the importance of getting their money to work for them by investing it safely.

I taught the difference between simple and compound interest and why they needed to increase their financial literacy if they planned to win the money game. The topic of profits being better than wages was thoroughly covered and real estate investing and business ownership were used to provide concrete examples of the concept.

To bring things to their level of understanding, we discussed the various ways they earned money at home and what other services they might provide to the community to earn money. At the end of four weeks, the students were given a quiz.

I asked the students to tell me what they would do if I gave them $20.00. The first student put up his hand and shared that he would save his money by putting it in the bank. He was quite proud of himself, and I congratulated him and told him that his idea was sound.

A second student said he would buy a very expensive battery that would allow him to play his video game longer. I was not expecting this response, and was a little disappointed with his answer; but at 13 years of age he can be excused for placing greater importance on his video games than understanding how money works. At the age of 13 we might excuse him for his lack of understanding.

Finally a young man named Romeo spoke up, and the other students all turned to listen. He was a very quiet student who would often ask additional questions or share some of the things he did to earn money after my lessons were over.

"What would you do with your $20.00, Romeo?"

"Mr. Carroll based on what you have taught us I would buy a shovel."

"Why is that?" I asked, already knowing the answer as I had shared with the class that I shoveled driveways to earn money when I was their age.

"I would go to the wealthy neighbourhoods and ask if I could shovel their driveways."

"So what would you do with that money?"

"Well you told us profits are better than wages, so I would reinvest it and buy two other shovels."

"Then what?"

"I would ask my friends if they wanted a job and have them shovel with me, but I would only pay them a portion of what I would get for getting the work done, because these were my contracts."

I was beaming. Here was a 12-year-old who really understood what I had been saying. He understood the importance of reinvesting into his business in order to grow. He understood that not only can you leverage money, but you can leverage people. He knew he could only be in one place at a time, and that therefore the income he earned singlehandedly would be limited. By expanding his business and giving his friends jobs he was able to be in more than one place at a time. He was able to increase his income, not by working twice as hard, but by working twice as smart.

Romeo was now an employer, in a position to get favourable tax treatment as a business owner and claim his employees' salaries as a business expense.

If this 12-year-old boy could see the light after a six-week course, what's stopping you? You have all the ability, all the resources, all the time you need to chart a different course for a brighter tomorrow. All you have to do is take the wheel. You are the captain of your own ship and fully in control of the journey ahead. You were born for greatness. Take steps now to create the life you deserve to live.

Successful people have known all along that wealth is created through the profits they make and not by income in the form of a wage or salary. This is one reason they look for opportunities to create multiple streams of income to build their wealth. And so should you. The more profit streams you have, the quicker you climb to the top of the financial ladder. So let's take a closer look at the three vehicles you will need to drive to your financial success.

Chapter Ten

Business Ownership

I f you are a serious reader and a fan of Robert Kiyosaki, you're probably familiar with his bestselling book *Cashflow Quadrant*, part of his *Rich Dad, Poor Dad* series. If you are not acquainted with his work and the real estate empire he has built, I strongly recommend that you get yourself a copy of that book as soon as you've finished reading this one.

In *Cashflow Quadrant*, Kiyosaki describes how his rich dad drew him a diagram (to which the book's title refers) showing the four different types of people who make up the business world. It was the very first time I had heard of this diagram. It was a powerful eye-opener, highlighting not only how the truly successful in business generated their wealth, but more importantly, how they managed to keep it for the long term. I knew I had to find a way to get to the best corner of the quadrant. Take a close look at the quadrant, if you are operating from the right side you are doing what is needed to have cash-flow coming in and time-freedom rolling out.

The Cashflow Quadrant

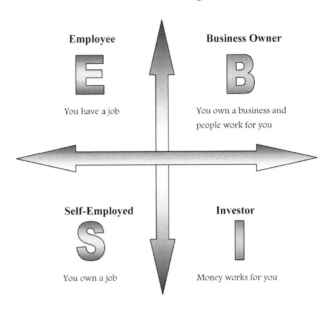

- **E — Employee.** Upper left of the quadrant. This person is looking for a safe, secure job with benefits. Type E's core value is job security. By now you and I know there is no such thing; it is only an illusion, especially with the cloud of economic uncertainty that continues to hover over us. And yet this is still where the majority in society spend their energy.
- **S — Self-Employed or Solo.** Lower left of the quadrant. Type S is the small business owner or the self-employed, whose core values are summed up as "If you want it done right, do it yourself." Generally a one-person act, this type of person goes it alone, with little or no leverage in their business model. There are many high-income earners in this group (think of your dentist, doctor, lawyer, etc.), but they are still trading a tremendous amount of time for money.
- **B — Business Owner.** Upper right of the quadrant. Unlike those in the S quadrant, type B people look for ways to use leverage to their advantage. They don't try to do things on their own; they build systems to support their business operations and look for the best possible people to run their companies. Putting this book together, I spent many hours writing in our local Tim Hortons. At one point I asked the store manager if

I could speak with the owners. "Good luck, honey" was her reply. "You won't ever see them here." The core value driving the business owner is time freedom and financial freedom.

- **I — Investor.** Lower right of the quadrant. **This is where we all secretly want to be, but only a very small minority ever get here.** Type I people have learned how to build businesses and take the income generated from those businesses to create true and lasting wealth. In other words, they make money work for them and have left the rat race for the playground of the rich.

As you may notice, the left side of the quadrant, comprising E and S, is reserved for those who trade time for money, and the right side, comprising B and I, is for those who would rather free up their time and have money work for them. There is nothing wrong with living your life on the left side if you so choose. In fact, I would say the majority of people in society don't mind the daily 9-to-5 grind; as long as they can pay the bills at the end of the month they are quite content. Although the right side of the quadrant can lead to financial freedom and time freedom, it is not for everyone. You need to have a wealth-creation mindset or you will never take the action needed to move from the left side to the right side.

However, if you want more in your life, you have to find ways of earning some of your income from the right side of the quadrant. So how do you do this? You must find a way to generate multiple streams of income.

What do you think of when you hear "multiple streams of income"? Do you think of another pitch from someone trying to recruit you to join their internet or multi-level marketing business? Do you think of representatives selling you on the merits of their company only to unload merchandise on you that not even your mother would buy? Maybe you've thought about becoming a franchisee so you wouldn't have to work and could spend your days sipping margaritas on the beach. If you are anything like me, then all these things have crossed your mind.

When my brother was alive, he had gotten himself hooked up with a multi-level marketing company that sold water filters. He was promised the world and told that even if he didn't recruit anyone he would be able to make a good income just by selling the products. These filters were not like those you and I are now accustomed to, but a complex system of hoses and canisters. The canister sat under your sink or on your counter. One arm of the hose would run from the canister to your kitchen pipe and the other arm had a valve that allowed you to filter water when you needed it.

My brother was a smooth talker, but not even his charm could help him sell those things. Not only were the filters expensive, but they were cumbersome and inconvenient as well. To make matters worse, he had to take possession and store the physical items in the house. Within a month he had lost all confidence in making money in his new business venture.

When I started assessing where I was in my financial life, I knew I had to do more but didn't know what. Remembering my brother's failed experience, I had no desire to test the MLM (multi-level marketing) idea. So I decided to look at different franchise opportunities to see if they might be my ticket to the right side of the quadrant.

I knew from all my reading that the majority of those who were doing well financially owned a business of some kind. But as I did my research I found that the entry price for owning a franchise was way out of my league. Not only was money an issue, but I knew absolutely nothing about running a business. I also knew that far more people had failed in business than those who had succeeded. Business ownership is definitely one pillar to wealth, but you need to be aware of some pros and cons:

Pros

- Small business owners are more likely to have high incomes.
- You call the shots. You decide (when formulating your goals) how much money you want to make, when you want to work, under what conditions you want to work, and who you want to work with. You also determine your success.
- Many government grants are available for budding entrepreneurs.
- Small business owners can put away up to $30,000 in pre-tax dollars into retirement accounts. This allows more money to grow under compounding interest before you have to pay taxes on any of it. If you are not a small business owner, the amount of pre-tax dollars that you can put in a retirement account is much less.
- Tax advantages are available to you that are not given to employees.

- Small business owners usually find great satisfaction in creating products or services and solving problems required to get those products and services into the market.

Cons

- Owning a small business involves a great deal of risk and in some cases a great deal of capital. Because small business owners are usually heavily invested personally, they stand to lose personal assets if the business fails.
- Bureaucracy. Small business owners deal with taxes, healthcare issues, and loads of paperwork. They must adhere to strict regulations that the federal, provincial, and municipal governments impose on them. However, unlike a corporation, a small business usually has a very limited number of people available to deal with all the red tape.
- Small business ownership involves a life full of change. Life changes dramatically when you first start up, of course, but markets and the economy are constantly changing also. Small businesses have to keep pace and be able to offer a viable product or service.
- While being your own boss can be liberating, it is also a position full of responsibility. Many small business owners struggle with the fine line between work and home. Other small business owners find that they just can't handle the stress that goes with so much responsibility.
- Competition can be intense between small businesses. Staying competitive is critical to your success.

Each of you will have to weigh the pros and cons of entry. For many business owners the positives of being able to write their own paycheque and build a solid financial house greatly outweigh any negatives. Small business is the engine that keeps our economy running and is responsible for creating thousands of jobs in the private sector.

Some of you have great ideas for a business that could unlock the door to a brighter financial future and have not acted. For some, your failure to act is driven by fear of the unknown, or concern that someone might already have had your idea or done what it is you are thinking of doing. What you need to remember is that there are no new ideas in this world. Those that have consumed your thoughts have also been planted in the minds of others. The universe loves speed, and it is the speed of your execution that will often determine the level of your success. Owning your own business is not easy, and it certainly isn't for everyone, but fortunately other, less demanding options can be quite profitable.

Multi-level marketing (MLM)

I have mentioned my hesitation to pursue the opportunities available in the multi-level marketing (MLM) industry because of my brother's personal experience. But after seeing the high cost to purchase a franchise, and not having any knowledge in the field of business, I decided to give it another look. The good news for you and me is that the MLM business has changed dramatically since my brother made his first attempt in the early 1980s.

Today there are countless legitimate revenue-generating opportunities out there to meet every individual's personal disposition. What I have grown to like about this form of business is that the cost for entry is usually quite reasonable and can easily be afforded by almost everyone.

If you are not familiar with multi-level marketing, let me explain.

MLM relies on network marketing, which is essentially building a distribution model. This is in contrast to the traditional business model, in which manufacturers have to spend millions of dollars to reach consumers through many different levels of distribution channels and by massive advertising. The network marketing model is able to reach consumers via one level of distribution (independent distributors), saving tremendously on sales, marketing, and advertising. That money is then put back into R&D (research and development), higher-quality products, and ultimately creating wealth for distributors and better profitability for the company.

MLM involves direct selling of products and services through the personal recommendation and endorsement of independent representatives. In return for your personal recommendation and endorsement, you receive a commission on the sale. It's different from a normal business in that it doesn't have a storefront, and you generally won't see the product or service being advertised in the mainstream media.

The business model is largely based on independent representatives recruiting or "sponsoring" other independent representatives to also direct-sell products and services. These sub-representatives would then make up your down-line. As the sponsor of these independent representatives, you receive a commission on the sales they make, as well as your own.

Similarly, your sponsor, and their sponsors, form your up-line and receive a commission on the sales made by you and your down-line.

For many people, this type of business has become their main source of income, because it offers many advantages over both the 9-to-5 opportunity sought by the masses and the ownership of a typical small business. These advantages were compelling enough for me that I took the plunge and joined Primerica Financial Services in 2004. Some of the advantages are listed below.

Advantages of the MLM Industry

Low Barriers to Entry

A particular strength of the MLM industry is that it provides equal opportunity for anyone who wishes to get involved. There are no post-secondary entry requirements like a college or university degree to serve as barriers for entry. All that is required is a desire to own your own business and build it from the ground up.

The financial cost to set up your business compared to other small business/franchise start-ups is relatively low in most situations. However, some MLMs will require an additional monthly cost in addition to your start-up cost, so you will need to do your own research.

Product Storage Not Required

MLM companies understand that their representatives are looking for convenience when it comes to running their business. Gone are the days when you had to take physical possession of products in order to sell them. Today you are selling an already manufactured product that is drop-shipped to your customers once a sale is made. This means all you need to do is focus on building your team and making sales.

Flexible Hours

When I was considering a multi-level marketing company, I knew it had to be in the financial services because I wanted to correct the errors my family and I had made. The trouble was that few companies offered flexibility when it came to part-time opportunities, and this was important to me. I loved my job as a teacher and wasn't about to give up a full-time salary hoping to make it big elsewhere. Primerica offered part-time opportunities to its representatives and I took it. Today, most MLM businesses offer part-time opportunities to independent representatives. This is good for you the representative, but even better for the companies as they gain increased numbers of representatives pushing their products and services. The bottom line is everyone wins.

A word of caution, as an independent rep, you have no one to report to but yourself. Beware of the temptation to treat these opportunities like a hobby, as doing so will not bring you the financial rewards you seek.

Leveraged Income

"Leveraged" simply means you receive a continuing benefit from a single initial effort. Because you're earning commissions on sales generated by your down-line as well as your own sales, you will continue to make an income as long as your down-line works hard. This is why recruiting is such a critically important component of this business model. The key to success in any MLM business is to recruit superstars who will go on to build massive legs below you. Success in this will bring a nice stream of continual income to your bank account.

Pre-existing System

Along with not having to come up with a marketing plan for your business, you don't need to reinvent the wheel when it comes to systems for recruiting, or developing and training your down-line. These are already established by the MLM companies you are representing. They have spent millions of dollars researching what works and what doesn't, so you can hit the ground running and start earning money quickly.

Who Should Consider This Opportunity?

If you are not where you had hoped to be in your financial life and have considered additional streams of income, MLM might very well be for you. Many people still believe MLMs are scams and that there is no money to be made in this industry. This could not be further from the truth. I have friends who have successfully made the transition from their regular 9-to-5 jobs and are now earning more money with their MLM business than they did in their previous jobs.

That said; this industry is not for everyone. For one thing you will need to be a self-starter who is able to lead others. You will need to believe passionately in the products and services you are promoting, or you will not be able to recruit others to your cause or make the sales needed to increase your income. Once you have recruited enough people for your down-line, you need to stay in touch with them and provide consistent support, guidance, and leadership. However, if your business is going to grow you need to give most of your time to those who deserve it and not to those who need it.

You must, of course, be a people person with good communication skills. You should have a pleasant and outgoing personality. This doesn't mean only face to face, many MLM opportunities are exclusively run on the internet, making it unnecessary to meet most of the people you work with on a daily basis. Nevertheless, this is a skill that you want to improve because it can only add value to what you are offering.

What You Should Look for in a Company

As you might imagine, not all MLM businesses are created equal. Although the industry has undergone many changes and improvements over the past two decades, you will need to do some careful homework to choose the right company.

There are three key criteria for recognizing a company that ensures longevity and long-term passive residual income:

1. The company is over 20 years old.
2. It has over $1 billion in sales.
3. It is regulated by government and provides transparency to the public.

Many solid companies fit these criteria. One that I really like in this respect is Nu Skin, an industry leader in both skin care and nutrition.

Here are some reasons why the Nu Skin business opportunity has been a top choice for many successful people to create additional income and wealth, and why it could very well be perfect for you:

1. There is currently a mega trend toward anti-aging products that has created huge demand in the marketplace. This is a $200 billion market that will only increase due to our aging baby boomers.

2. Nu Skin was started in 1984 and has a proven and solid track record, and now operates in 52 countries.

3. Nu Skin was named "one of the world's fastest-growing public companies" and is listed on the NYSE. It has a rich compensation plan, creating one million-dollar earner every five days.

For the record, I am not a representative of Nu Skin Inc. — but I do have their stock in my portfolio because I am impressed by what the company has achieved in the industry. To find out if this company is right for you, connect with my good friend Excelle Liu at excelle_liu@ yahoo.com, or visit her website at www.excelle.nsopportunity.com to learn more.

Finally, remember that the MLM industry is a very personal way of selling. You will need to exercise your own powers of persuasion and influence to encourage others to come on board with you. If you are going to do this successfully, you must have 100% commitment to the program and services you are promoting. If you do not firmly believe in what your company stands for or is offering, do not get involved. There can be nothing worse than promoting something that you yourself are not genuinely committed to, just to make a few dollars. You might be able to fool a few clients here and there, and possibly some members on your team; but the truth will eventually be revealed, leaving you exposed as someone who lacks integrity.

Although I would still classify MLMs as an E on the Cashflow Quadrant, they do provide some tax benefits and additional income streams not given to traditional employees. Whether you decide on a traditional business opportunity or choose to take your chances with an MLM company, you owe it to yourself to do all you can to secure your financial future.

Chapter Eleven

Stock Market

et me begin this section by stating for the record that I am not a financial advisor, nor do I hold myself out as someone with knowledge of the stock market and how to safely invest to maximize your returns. I am merely a messenger sharing my stories and explaining the insights I've gathered over the past seven years while trying to put my financial house in order. The material in this book, and especially in this section, is based solely on opinions gathered from my personal experience, along with information obtained from courses and seminars. I would strongly advise you to do your own research when deciding on which vehicle to safely drive to your financial destination.

For many people the stock market has a certain allure and sense of adventure about it. Some see it as the ultimate challenge of their intellectual ability, and will spend an inordinate amount of time doing technical and fundamental analysis in order to choose the stocks that will ultimately help them make a killing. These individuals believe they have the skills and knowledge needed to consistently beat the market, and will often choose stocks as their vehicle to wealth. The sad truth is that no one has a crystal ball when it comes to predicting how the markets will behave. None of the so-called gurus who write financial newsletters or the pundits on CNBC and BNN can predict with certainty what will happen a month from now, let alone a few years from now. Trying to beat the market is a fallacy, because the market always wins.

Some see the stock market as a dangerous and risky business to be avoided at all costs. The constant volatility, with the S&P, TSX, and DOW going up one day, only to be down by hundreds the next, is not a place for those with weak stomachs. The increased volatility of the past few years has left millions with a large portion of their retirement income depleted. And although some have been able to regain some of their losses by staying invested during the tough times, the vast majority of investors have not. The financial crisis of 2007 and the carnage it left in its wake lent additional support to this group of individuals who believe stocks should be avoided, period.

Still, there are others who see investing in the stock market as only one of many vehicles to be used in the pursuit of their financial goals. They don't fear putting their money into solid companies that have generated both growth and income over the years. They avoid speculation and will not put all their eggs in one basket in the vain hope of hitting one out of the park. For this group, diversification and asset allocation is the rule when it comes to sound investing for their brighter financial futures. They are disciplined and often follow a system for when to buy and sell stocks in order to protect their principal from loss. This group understands that stocks have performed better than other asset classes in providing superior long-term returns. They are patient and look for safe consistent returns by investing in companies that consistently increase earnings. Earnings are the net profits of a business, and companies that consistently increase earnings year after year will see their stock prices grow in lockstep.

So what kind of investor are you? The answer to that question will be determined by your tolerance for risk, along with your personal philosophy. For me, investing in the stock market is a deadly serious business, and a place I can least afford to be reckless with my money. In 2007 and 2008 I thought making money in stocks would be a piece of cake. Without any training except a home study course I had purchased and studied for six months, I made the decision to dive in head first with the intent of making a huge killing. But the only thing that got killed was my pride, and my bank account to the tune of several thousand dollars.

Not only did I pick the absolute worst time to enter the market (on the heels of the stock market crash), but my research skills were unsound and grossly inadequate. I didn't understand that wealth, like all things worth having, takes time.

Today I am a very different investor, with a better understanding of how to successfully trade the market. I will share some of the strategies I have learned since my earlier errors, and hope that they will be of help to you; but before doing that, I will give you a close look at the pros and cons of investing in the stock market.

Stock Market Pros

Many people love buying shares of individual stocks, mutual funds, or exchange traded funds (ETFs), because it gives them part-ownership in a company or group of companies. The more shares you own, the greater your percentage of ownership in that particular company. In the interest of time I will not get into the definition of these terms. However, a quick Google search will provide you with all the answers you need.

One advantage of owning stocks is that you can purchase shares of companies with very little money. [**A stock (also known as equity or a share) is a portion of the ownership of a corporation. A share in a corporation gives the owner of the stock a stake in the company and its profits. If a corporation has issued 100 shares in total, then each share represents a 1% ownership in the company**]. Most of us don't have the capital or the experience to run our own business. But those with the most modest means can own a stake in a profitable business by investing in stocks. Had you bought a few shares of Apple in the late 1990s you would have earned the same returns as the late great Steve Jobs. Bottom line: the stock market allows the little guy to run with the big dogs.

Ease of entry

Purchasing shares is quite easy to do and can be done from anywhere in the world once you are connected to the internet. Here are two simple ways to get started. Let's say you want to buy a few hundred shares in Microsoft. What you will need to do is open up a trading account. One solution is to speak with the broker at one of your financial institutions and have them set up a trading account for you. All banks have a trading platform to assist those who would rather do their own trading instead of relying on a broker. Once this is done you can transfer funds to your trading account and purchase the shares you want.

A second method is to shop online for a discount broker. The advantage of this method over dealing with your bank is that the fees for buying and selling your stocks are often discounted beyond what your banks will charge you. This will have a significant impact on your account balance if you do a lot of trading. Be forewarned that you will need to do your homework so that you don't get charged ridiculously high commission fees on every trade you make.

Liquidity

Another positive of owning stocks is that it is a very liquid asset class. You can cash out with relative ease, and your money can be in your hands within a few business days. Many people like this, as it gives them peace of mind should they need money in an emergency or feel they just can't stomach the volatility in the markets any longer. If your retirement money is invested in a registered account, you must resist the temptation of cashing out for so-called emergencies. Buying a car with your retirement savings is not a good idea. I have had clients make this colossal mistake only to regret such a move shortly after. You should set up another account to meet life's emergencies, but don't tap your retirement account and other money that is growing tax-deferred.

No Ceiling on Returns

The stock market has the potential to bring you a phenomenal rate of return and make you rich if you buy into the right company at the right time. Just imagine if you had bought $20,000 of Apple shares in 1995 when the stock price was $5.95. By February 2012, your investment would be worth a cool $1,408,695.65. It is easy to see why so many millions play the market hoping to land the next Apple or Google in their portfolios.

Professional Advisors

You don't need to understand all the technical and analytical jargon spoken in this space in order to invest in the stock market. There are professional advisors out there who would be more than happy to provide advice and guidance to you for a small fee. They will manage your portfolio and make decisions about which stocks to buy and sell. Some are very good at what they do, but sadly the majority will end up losing your money. Nonetheless, many people like this idea, because all they have to do is transfer funds and the money manager will take care of the rest. As I have mentioned before, no one cares more about your money than you, so I would think twice before turning my money over to someone else to manage.

Tax Benefits

You can defer your taxes by purchasing stocks inside your RRSP. You will not pay taxes on the equity appreciation until you decide to take out the money. This allows time and compounding to work for you and grow your wealth.

Canadians can also invest up to $5,000 a year into their Tax Free Savings Account (TSFA) with after-tax dollars. **[A TSFA is an account that does not charge taxes on any interest earned, dividends or capital gains, and the money can be withdrawn tax free at any time. The contributions are not tax deductible and any unused room can be carried forward and is available to adults 18 years or older].**

Because the growth from this account is exempt from taxes, it provides Canadians with an additional tax-advantaged account to grow their wealth.

Stock Market Cons

Returns Not Guaranteed

Unlike GICs, bonds, and Treasury bills, there are no guarantees that your principal will be protected when you invest in the stock market. There is greater risk associated with putting your money into equities. Of course, the flip side of risk is great reward — there is no limit to how high a stock can climb over time. That is great news, but you can also lose everything you've invested. Those with a low tolerance for risk and uncertainty usually avoid putting their money into the markets.

Zero Control

Unlike real estate, GICs, and some MLM businesses, you have absolutely no control over the performance of your investment. Economic concerns in one part of the world (think Europe) can have adverse effects on how your stocks perform so can wars and political instability. If you are the type of individual who seeks 100% control of your investments you will not find it in the stock market.

Fees and More Fees

One of the challenges of investing is finding a vehicle where your money can safely and consistently return a profit. The whipsaw stock market we have seen over the past several years makes this task more and more difficult with each passing day. What is even more disturbing are the outrageous fees being charged by advisors and portfolio managers who for the most part significantly underperform the market. I believe in paying for value, but the fees being charged by mutual fund companies and portfolio managers should be illegal, especially in the Canadian market. Many people would be much better off ditching these high fee and commission structures in order to safeguard more of their money. The question is where do you go? Not to worry, I will share a better strategy with you in a few short paragraphs.

No Power to Leverage

There is zero leverage available for the average investor to purchase shares. If you want to buy $50,000 worth of ABC Company, you will need to have $50,000 in your account (excluding options and buying on margin). Coming up with $50,000 or even $20,000 to jumpstart your retirement plan would require years of sacrifice and disciplined saving for the average person. But if this is your vehicle and you are behind the eight-ball when it comes to a sizable investment for your retirement, you don't have any other options. The banks won't assume the majority of the risk for your stocks as they would for a hard asset like real estate. Therefore, you will need to save more (a lot more) for as long as you can, and begin as early as you can.

It is true that investors can use leverage to purchase stocks by buying options and or buying on margin, but I would not recommend beginners do so. For one thing these strategies involve a considerable amount of risk of suffering serious financial loss in a very short period of time. Secondly this book is about minimizing risk and growing your wealth safely by taking advantage of the power of time and compounding. To promote high risk investment practises and explain them with sufficient details for you the reader falls outside my area of expertise and the purpose for which this book was written.

Learn the Basics

Investing safely does not require you to have the intellect of an Einstein, but it does require you to do your homework and learn some basics so that no one pulls the wool over your eyes. After all, it is your money, and you should invest in your own knowledge so you know how to protect and keep your money safe.

Having a high intellect has absolutely no correlation with stock market success. Einstein, one of the greatest minds of all time, failed miserably in the stock market, even losing his Nobel Prize money on bad investment decisions. All you need in order to be successful in the market is basic understanding of financial matters, a proven system that works and patience and discipline to avoid the emotions of fear and greed.

There are many compelling reasons both for and against investing in the stock market and each of us must decide if it is worth using to achieve our financial goals. Many people invest in the stock market because over time it has proven quite rewarding.

Sadly, there is no proven formula that will ensure your trades are successful. And with the current market volatility we can probably expect to see stocks up one day and down the next for some time to come. But don't let this dissuade you from putting your money in the markets. When done correctly, this vehicle to wealth can bring you consistently solid returns over the long term and reward you handsomely for your patience.

Contrary to the noise you hear from advisors and brokers on the news channels, investing does not have to be complicated. In fact, it is quite simple when you get away from all the noise and strip it down to its bare bones. As an investor you are looking for simple and easy, not sexy and complicated. The latter might sound good and exciting, but it also brings increased risk of losing your shirt.

The stock market can reward you if you proceed with caution and have a system. A system may not always bring you winners, but having one ensures that you take emotions out of the picture and make decisions with your head.

Let me now share two strategies that have been used successfully for investing in the stock market. They are both simple — some might even say boring – but they have proven quite effective in protecting one's principal and delivering consistent returns.

Avoid Speculation

There are two primary reasons why people lose money when trading: fear and greed. In short, they have the wrong psychological outlook for trading. They will get into a stock at the peak of its bull run because they are greedy to get in on something big. As soon as they buy the stock, other investors will start to take profits, reducing the share price. They will quickly sell the stock at a loss for fear of losing everything, only to find out a few days or weeks later that the stock is back to the original price they bought it at. Greed got them into the stock and fear got them out, and the end result is they ended up losing much of their principal.

People who win when investing in the stock market usually follow a system, learn from the best, stay disciplined, lower their risk, and have clarity and focus for what they want to achieve.

Having the correct trading psychology is a key ingredient for success. With the right outlook you take control of fear and impulsiveness, learning to trade with your head. You might want to consider doing your trades after the markets are closed to protect yourself from your own emotions. Not only does this eliminate the emotion from your decision, but it allows you to do research and make an informed decision on each trade.

Another key ingredient that cannot be overlooked is managing your risk. Remember capital preservation is more important than the hope of capital appreciation. If you don't protect your capital, you will be out of the market in short order, wondering how in the world you didn't see that two-by-four coming full speed at your head. The stock market can be cruel and unforgiving, so you need to have a system for entry and exit.

If you are going to have success in the markets you will need to exercise both patience and discipline. Patience will be needed to stay in the market when your stock is trending higher and not take profits too early. Discipline will be needed to stick with a system that works and not get emotionally attached to a stock when the market trends down.

When I first started investing I felt that investments that didn't promise a return of at least 10% weren't worth my time. So I read the financial papers and listen to the talking heads on BNN for their recommendations on companies poised to outperform, hoping to see their share prices increase by 15% or more. I can tell you with 100% certainty that this strategy did not bring the big windfall I was looking for.

Here are the facts, and you would do well to highlight this section for future reference. ***The stock market never loses.*** Sure, it might be up one year only to be down the next, but when you analyze what is really happening you can see that the stock market level is just an indication of the average returns of all traders in the market.

Think back to your grade seven math class for a minute. Do you recall how your teacher came up with the average mark for the class? They took the best test scores and added them to the worst test scores, then divided by the number of students who wrote the test. As a student your goal was to score better than the class average or at the very least match it. We definitely did not want to score below average, as we automatically equated this with poor performance, regardless of how high the class average was. For us, getting the class average meant we were doing well and could rationalize to our parents that we were keeping pace with the majority of students.

Just like your junior class math average, the stock market is an index or benchmark that gives an account of the average performance of all investors in the market. This benchmark is used by individual investors and institutional investors to gauge whether they had a successful year. Every investor hopes to beat the index or the average return of the stock market, but this is a mathematical impossibility. Some investors will have to underperform the market and others will have to outperform the market in order to get an average for the market.

We all want to buy low and sell high in order to outperform the markets, but the majority of retail investors (you and I) end up buying high and selling low because we make our investment decisions based on speculative impulses and not sound principles.

History has shown clear statistical evidence that the majority of people underperform the markets by a considerable amount. More than 75% of the advisors on Wall Street (the guys with the fancy computers and up-to-the-minute market information) underperform the market. These are supposed to be the best of the best at picking stocks, yet only one-quarter of them manage to match or outperform the index.

So what about you and me? How do we stack up against those who are paid big money to get this thing right for their clients? Can we honestly expect to do better than the professional advisors on Wall Street? Many believe they can, but the truth is that about 90% of retail investors (the small guy like you and me) underperform the market regularly.

Wow! Stop and think about that for a minute. If you were asked to hand over your money to someone in a simple game of basketball in which your chance of beating your opponent was only one in ten, would you do it? Of course not, you would let logic rule the day and your decision would be an easy one to make.

But something peculiar happens to the majority of us when it comes to investing. We lose our ability to think logically and make good financial decisions with our money. We know the market is a system that cannot be beaten and we clearly understand that the odds are stacked against us. Yet millions of people continue to be led down the path of financial disaster believing they have the unique ability to be among the 10% of investors who occasionally get things right from time to time. Do you really believe you are that good?

So if the market always wins, why don't more investors try to match the performance of index funds to safely grow their money? I believe you already know the answer to that question. It starts with the letter G and ends with D — can you guess? It is our greed to have it all immediately that continues to consume our emotions and cause us to do foolish things with our money.

With that in mind, let's take a close look at why it pays to invest in index funds.

Buying the Index makes Dollars and Cents

Several years ago I was putting money away toward my retirement by buying mutual funds. [**Mutual Funds are an investment vehicle that pools money from many different investors to invest in stocks, bonds, or other assets. Typically, there are thousands (if not millions) of different investors who own shares of that mutual fund**]. I was sold the idea that the fund manager had successfully beaten the returns of the stock market four years in a row and was the best of the best.

Note: *When it comes to investing there is very little correlation between a fund manager's past success record and his future success.*

Not knowing this particular fact at the time, I decided to shell out my money, waiting impatiently to pocket the better-than-average returns that were sure to come. The first year was awesome, as my portfolio grew 15%, but that was the end of the party. The next six years were lean, and the returns came nowhere close to the first year's highs. Not only did they not come close to matching the highs, but the average performance of my portfolio grossly underperformed the market averages.

To say I was not happy would be an understatement. To me, the only thing worse than losing my money, is someone else losing my money for me. So I decided to take matters into my own hands and self-direct my RSP. I certainly couldn't do any worse. Or so I thought.

Like so many well-intentioned novice investors, I made the mistake of believing I could time the market and buy individual stocks to grow my wealth. What a rude awakening that was! It didn't take more than a few months for my principal to start evaporating.

Unlike mutual funds, where your investment dollars are used to buy shares in a number of different companies, diversifying your portfolio and reducing the volatility of your holdings, individual stocks offer no such protection. They leave you naked and vulnerable to every cold and or sniffles the stock market catches, and this can significantly erode the years of savings you have put away for your future. Anyone who tells you they have a winning strategy for picking individual stocks should be avoided at all cost. These individuals are speculators and not real investors. They are willing to lay big money on the line hoping to score the next Google in their portfolio.

A much better strategy for protecting your serious money would be to buy no-load mutual funds that are indexed or exchange-traded funds (ETFs,) for your portfolio. [**An exchange-traded fund is one that tracks an index but can be traded just like a stock. ETFs always bundle together the securities in an index, giving you access to a large number of companies in your portfolio**]. These funds can be bought and sold on the stock exchange throughout the day. They are not actively managed, so you will need to open up a trading account with an online broker or your bank.

ETFs have grown in popularity with investors over the past several years and offer a host of benefits not previously seen with traditional mutual funds. For starters they differ on a fundamental level from mutual funds in that you can trade them at anytime throughout the day. Conversely although mutual funds take orders during the trading hours, the transactions actually take place at the close of the market. The price you receive is the sum of the closing day prices of all the stocks in the fund. This is not the case for ETFs, which trade instantaneously all day long and allow an investor to lock in a price for the underlying stocks immediately. For regular traders this makes more sense when it comes to protecting their money when the market turns south or when taking profits at a price they want.

Another big advantage for ETFs is that they are economical to buy and maintain over the long-run. This is especially attractive to the buy-and-hold investor. Annual fees for ETF can be as low as 0.5%, which is breathtakingly low compared to the average mutual fund fees of 2.8%. As mentioned earlier, investors will have to pay a brokerage transaction fee with each purchase but with discount brokers this becomes negligible on sizable trades.

One more advantage worth noting when buying ETFs is that there are no sales loads or investment minimums like what you find with mutual funds. This means the average investor can keep more money in his pocket at the end of the day. This is a very important point to consider when it comes to your investments and your total returns.

Asset Allocation – Diversification for Profit

Let me share with you another strategy I found to be particularly effective in minimizing my losses and growing my money. After failing to get the investment returns I had hoped from buying individual stocks, I turned to a financial newsletter put out by the Oxford Club. A good friend who had benefited greatly from its advice recommended it to me.

Having nothing to lose, I decided to do some research on the Oxford Club. It revealed that the investment director of this publication, Mr. Alexander Green, had more than 20 years' experience on Wall Street as a portfolio manager, research analyst, investment advisor, and financial writer. Most importantly, the fund that he directed was ranked third in the United States for risk-adjusted returns over the past five years.

His market winning strategy had returned 11.4% annually since its inception in 2003 to thousands of his subscribers. I wanted to learn more about Mr. Alexander Green, and decided to buy his book *The Gone Fishin' Portfolio.*

As I've said, past performance does not guarantee similar future returns, but a track record like this required further exploration. What I learned from my reading of the book and his monthly newsletter is that the Gone Fishin' Portfolio was deceptively simple and easy to implement. There was nothing sexy or exciting about it, and that is a good thing for retail investors like you and me.

The strategy is based on the Nobel Prize–winning work in economics of Harry Markowitz, Merton Miller, and William Sharpe in 1990. Markowitz' groundbreaking paper "Portfolio Selection," published in *The Journal of Finance,*[20] laid the groundwork for much of today's asset allocation strategies.

Once you have finished this book, I suggest you pick up Alexander Green's book and read it in its entirety. It is not a difficult read, and the

---

20   Markowitz, Harry. Journal of Finance, "Portfolio Selection." Last modified March 1952. http://gacetafinanciera.com/TEORIARIESGO/MPS. pdf.

information you gather from it has the power to improve your financial future.

A Winning Strategy

The *Gone Fishin' Portfolio* is based on an asset allocation model and has two primary goals. One is to help you earn a higher rate of return within acceptable risk, and the second is to save you time and simplify your life so you can do the things you have always dreamed of doing.

The asset allocation recommends having 30% of your money in U.S. stocks with 15% in large-cap and 15% in small-cap stocks. [**Large caps have a market capitalization of $5 billion or more; small caps have market capitalization of $3 billion or less**]. Market capitalization is determined by multiplying the number of shares outstanding by the share price.

Another 30% of your money is invested in bonds, with 10% going to three different types (*high-yield corporate funds, short-term investment-grade funds, and inflation-protected securities funds*).

The next 30% should be invested in *international stocks* with 10% in the Pacific Rim, 10% in emerging markets, and 10% in European stocks. Don't get tripped out about putting 10% of your investment dollars into Europe because of the current crisis. Remember, tough times don't last forever. The European market will rebound, and those who are invested will reap the rewards when it does.

The remaining 10% of your money should be split evenly with 5% in *precious metals* and the other 5% in *real estate investment trusts* (REITs).

The portfolio is made up of 10 Vanguard mutual funds. Why, you ask, would anyone hold 10 different mutual funds, especially when annual expenses are so high? This is a very good question but I found out that the Vanguard mutual funds have some of the lowest annual expenses in the market, as much as four times lower than other funds. The other thing to know about these funds is that they are not actively managed which saves you big-time on management expenses. Take a look at the following chart to see the cost savings when investing in Vanguard Funds and ETFs.

Vanguard Fees Verses ETF Fees Verses Industry Average

Vanguard Fund	ETF Alternative	Vanguard Fees	ETF Fees	Industry Average
Vanguard Total Stock Market Index (VTSMX)	Vanguard Total Stock Market (VTI)	0.23%	0.07%	1.43%
Vanguard Small Cap Index (NAESX)	Vanguard Small Cap (VB)	0.37%	0.10%	2.01%
Vanguard Emerging Market Index (VEIEX)	Vanguard European (VGK)	0.22%	0.12%	1.78%
Vanguard European Index (VEURX)	Vanguard Pacific (VPL)	0.18%	0.12%	1.00%
Vanguard Pacific Index (VPACX)	Vanguard Emerging Market (VWO)	0.20%	0.25%	1.54%
Vanguard High Yield Corporate (VWEHX)	iShares iBoxx High Yield Corporate Bond (HYG)	0.20%	0.50%	1.02%
Vanguard Short Term Investment Grade Bonds (VFSTX)	Vanguard Total Bond Market (BND)	0.22%	0.11%	1.70%
Vanguard Inflation Protected Securities (VIPSX)	iShares Lehman TIPs (TIP)	0.15%	0.20%	1.18%
Vanguard REIT Index (VGSIX)	Vanguard REIT (VNQ)	0.26%	0.12%	1.24%
Vanguard Precious Metals and Mining Fund (VGPMX)	Market Vectors Gold Miners (GDX)	0.28%	0.55%	1.64%

The one drawback to using this particular strategy is that the Vanguard Group of Funds requires a minimum investment of $3,000 per fund. This means you would need $30,000 to invest if you planned on using this specific strategy. If you are just getting started this might not be possible, however, don't be discouraged, the book outlines an ETF alternative that will deliver similar results.

As I get older, I continually look for ways to work smarter and not harder. In addition, I appreciate those who follow the **KISS** principle (*keep it short and simple*) when it comes to teaching about money and finance. One of the most refreshing things you will find about the *Gone Fishin' Portfolio* is that it is beautifully simple to implement. Once you have set things up and purchased your funds, all you need to do is sit back and relax.

I will admit this was extremely difficult for me to do at first, especially considering that the performance of my RSP was riding on this strategy. But I soon learned that I didn't need to check the markets daily and worry about my portfolio. Instead, I took comfort in the fact that the portfolio's asset allocation model is specifically built to match or exceed the return of being fully invested in stocks without enduring the hair-raising volatility of a 100% stock portfolio. It is designed to be both aggressive enough to boost your long-term returns and uncorrelated enough (to the broad market) to smooth out the inevitable bumps along the way. And believe me, there will be bumps. But what makes these bumps less noticeable is the second part of the strategy, *rebalancing*, which you will also need to put in place.

As investors we love seeing our stocks increase in price, as that is the goal of investing. When we start seeing winners in our portfolio, it is easy to get emotionally caught up and want to add to our winning positions and dump our losers. This is normal, but this is where the *Gone Fishin' Portfolio* runs contrary to what we are psychologically conditioned to do.

Once a year this strategy calls for you to "rebalance" your portfolio, and the great thing is it will only take you about 20 minutes to do.

Why rebalance? The percentage of each fund you own will change significantly depending on the performance of the financial markets. Stocks might be higher because of consumer confidence and good economic news, and bonds might be lower. Gold mining shares might have fallen, and emerging markets might have seen a significant uptrend. Your job is to bring your asset allocation back to the recommended percentages. Doing this controls risk and could boost your performance over the years.

Rebalancing requires you to reduce the amount you have invested in the best-performing asset classes and add to those that have underperformed. Since all assets move in cycles, rebalancing forces you to sell high and buy low. There are two ways to rebalance at the end of the year.

One way is to add new money into the asset classes that have underperformed until you achieve the right balance. This might be fine in the early years of using this model, but it will become more and more difficult as you watch your portfolio grow.

The second strategy is to reduce the position of your best-performing asset class by selling shares and redistributing that money to those that are out of balance. The one drawback, especially if you are using the ETF alternative, is that you will be charged commissions for each side of your trades. The second drawback is that you are not adding new money to your investment portfolio.

Regardless of which option you think is best for rebalancing, just make sure you do it. Don't get caught piling more money into the hottest stock at the end of the year. You must remain disciplined. Keep in mind that every asset class has its moment in the sun.

As mentioned, successful people are action-oriented. They do the research necessary when weighing decisions, and once they have seen the soundness of an idea, they act. I have shared with you a portfolio model that is easy to understand, implement, and manage. It has a very impressive track record, but at the end of the day your decisions must be the product of your own conclusions. I am not telling you to adopt this strategy I am merely sharing what I have used in the past. Take a look at the following chart. It compares the results of the S&P 500 Index against the *Gone Fishin' Portfolio* over the same time period.

When you add it all up the S&P has averaged a return of 7.47% over the course of the past nine years, compared to 11.4% for the *Gone Fishin' Portfolio*. Some of you might be thinking 4% is not a huge difference and you could not be further from the truth. If those are your thoughts, you have clearly forgotten the power of compounding. So let me refresh your memory.

Gone Fishin' Annual Returns Verses S&P Annual Returns, 2003–2010

Year	GFP	S&P 500
2003	32.72	28.68
2004	15.28	10.88
2005	11.93	4.91
2006	16.99	15.80
2007	10.75	5.49
2008	−31.7	−37.0
2009	34.3	23.4
2010	16.1	15.1
2011	−3.19	0.0

Nobel Prize–winning physicist Albert Einstein once called the mathematical formula for calculating the investment returns and time needed for doubling our money — known as the "Rule of 72" — the greatest invention in history.

According to the Rule of 72, if you divide the number 72 by the interest rate you earn on an investment, this gives the number of years it would take for your money to double. Therefore, if we took the returns of the S&P and divided it into 72, your money would double every 9.6 years. However, if you divided 72 by the 11.4% of the *Gone Fishin' Portfolio*, your money would double in 6.3 years.

Here is the significance of what an extra 4% return on your money could do for your investment dollars. If you invested a lump sum of $20,000 in two different investment vehicles for 25 years, with one returning 7.5% and the other 11.4%, how would each of those investments do?

The investment returning 7.5% would double every 9.6 years or approximately 2.6x in 25 years. This means your $20,000 would be worth $52,000 in 25 years.

The investment returning 11.4% annually would have your money doubling every 6.3 years, or approximately 3.97x in 25 years. This means your $20,000 would be worth $79,000 in 25 years.

The rate of return on your investments will have a significant impact on the performance of your investments over the long run. You must do all you can to minimize unnecessary expenses that promise you great returns but in the end take money out of your pocket. Each of us must decide what vehicles, if any, we wish to drive to financial freedom. So far we have explored business ownership and the stock market, however the best strategy in my opinion is just around the next bend and that is real estate investing.

Chapter Twelve

Real Estate Investing

n my opinion nothing beats real estate investing when it comes to securing your financial future. It has the ability to transform an anaemic bank account to one that is strong and bulging. Some of the wealthiest men and women in society have attributed their wealth to their real estate purchases. In fact, *Fortune Magazine* recently reported that 97% of all wealth was either created or held in real estate. If you are serious about your financial fitness, you need to go where the results are.

But isn't real estate investing too risky? Like all vehicles to wealth, real estate does have its share of pros and cons. Yes, there are risks, but if you know what you are doing it is certainly not risky. In fact, I would say real estate is far less risky than starting your own business or putting your money into the stock market.

One of the biggest obstacles stopping most people from driving this vehicle to wealth is their belief that real estate investing is too expensive. True, the years of buying an investment property with only 5% down are long gone and not likely to return. However, even with the new requirements of 20%, it is possible for most working Canadians to afford the down payment for a property. It all depends on where you choose to look.

If you live in large metropolitan areas like Toronto or Vancouver, I would advise you to limit the amount of time spent researching these markets for cash-flow investment property, unless you have deep pockets and money is not a concern. The hot Toronto and Vancouver markets have inflated the average price of real estate, making it extremely difficult to find good value for your money. Instead I would advise you to set your sights on smaller real estate markets to find undervalued properties that generate cash-flow. For me this was the only option, since I had arrived late to the investment party. Buying real estate is a way of forced savings, ensuring that I put at least 20% of my annual income toward my future financial goals.

Another issue keeping many potential investors stuck at the starting block is the fear of dealing with tenants. This is a very real concern, and one that should not be treated lightly. The world is full of people who look to exploit others and get things for free. Having your units occupied by someone who has no intention of paying can be a major inconvenience, and often requires the intervention of the courts to get them out.

That said we can mitigate this risk by making sure prospective tenants go through a thorough screening process. This should include but not be limited to obtaining references from employers and former landlords, along with credit and criminal background checks. This won't prevent all the bad apples from getting themselves into your building, but it should reduce the risk. Although professional squatters are a concern for investors, they are few and far between and should not stop you from seriously considering this vehicle.

Another concern often raised is that real estate investing requires too much time and managing a building is too difficult. While you will be required to spend time learning about the business, this doesn't have to consume your every waking hour. If you can devote a few hours a week to your learning and research, that will be plenty to get you started on a part-time basis.

Like any business, the more time you spend learning, the better equipped you will be to make informed decisions. One of the quickest ways to decrease the learning curve needed is to find a real estate investment club near you and surround yourself with people already achieving success. These clubs are easy to find. All you have to do is get on your computer and Google "real estate investment clubs." If you can't find one, then you might want to take the bull by the horns and start your own.

I am often surprised when speaking to novice investors, or those considering investing in real estate, how much they want to be involved in the management of their building. Listen, when it comes to real estate investing, the last thing you want to do is manage your property. You are investing in real estate not only for financial freedom but for time freedom.

There are many competent individuals and management companies who will take care of your buildings for a small fraction of your monthly rents. This not only provides you with peace of mind, but also allows you to work on your business and not in your business.

Despite the countless opportunities available for achieving financial freedom, the majority of people will still manage to find a range of "insurmountable" obstacles that stop them from moving their lives forward. Resolve to be one of those who are enlightened enough to take advantage and seize the moment.

I could go on pointing out more reasons people might give for not investing in real estate, but what good would it do you? What you want is to understand the positives of investing in real estate.

A Seed is Planted

About six years ago, I paused to take stock of where I was in my financial life. I had bought and sold my first home in Whitby and was now living in the beautiful city of Scarborough. I didn't have a big, fancy home, but it was enough for my needs, and I felt good about the fact that I was paying down my mortgage ahead of schedule.

I had just been promoted to vice-principal with the Toronto District School Board and was making what most would consider a good income. Although I was making regular contributions to my RRSP, it was far less than the 20% suggested for attaining true financial freedom and the accumulated results of my retirement portfolio were far from stellar. I knew I had to do something different if I was going to secure the kind of lifestyle and retirement income I had envisioned.

I shared my thoughts about wanting to do more and leave a legacy with a few of my close friends, but surprisingly not everyone was supportive of my lofty goals. "Why can't you be content with what you have?" was the response of a particularly close friend. "You make a good income, have one of the best pension plans coming to you, and are already making a difference in your schools." I was completely thrown by my friend's remarks. I had expected him to be one of my strongest supporters.

I took this as a direct attack on my character. "Why should I be content and settle?" was my hot response. "I am definitely grateful for what I have accomplished to this point in my life, but why should I put the brakes on and be content when there is so much more I want to do? Your opinion of what constitutes enough might be okay for you and the life you wish to live, but it is not enough for me. You speak of me having a great pension when I retire, and that might be correct, but what if I don't wish to stay in the teaching profession for another 20 years — what then?"

Yes, the teacher's pension is one of the best, but I want to be in control of my future. I want to create a passive income stream that will be far greater than my pension earnings. Life is to be lived to the fullest, and I will not be like others who see opportunity and walk the other way. I would rather take the calculated risk knowing that at least I gave my best.

I was furious as I left my friend's house, and was more determined than ever to do more with the talents I was given and to never tap out.

A few months after that heated encounter, I was having a conversation with my good friend Sarah. I brought up the topic of real estate investing and how I would like to become an investor. A few days later, she introduced me to Robert Kiyosaki's *Rich Dad, Poor Dad*. I had never heard of this author, but I was fascinated by the story of his two dads and could not put the book down.

I thanked Sarah profusely, and asked whether she had other books by the same author. She brought me all she had, and I read each from cover to cover. Sarah didn't know that the seed of an idea had been planted, one that would germinate to consume my daily thoughts — the idea that if Kiyosaki could create financial freedom through real estate then I could do the same.

Rich Dad, Poor Dad awoke a hunger in me I didn't even know existed, and I was determined to find a way to create wealth for myself in order to teach it to others.

I started buying books on personal finance and real estate investing to add to my growing library, and I began attending weekly seminars to learn as much as I could about real estate and wealth. Pretty soon I started noticing the same familiar faces at the various seminars I was attending. These individuals had the same dreams and desires as I did, and they were committed to learning and growing to change their lives. I quickly formed friendships with a few of them to learn about their investment strategies and why real estate was their vehicle of choice for financial freedom.

I now share with you what I have learned about the business of real estate and why, hands down, I think it is the best vehicle for transforming your financial life.

The Pros of Real Estate Investing
Leverage

Unlike the stock market, real estate allows you to leverage other people's money (in our case the bank's) to grow your wealth. This is phenomenal, because with a sound investment strategy and a good credit score, the sky's the limit for what you can truly build.

Let me explain. You have worked very hard over the past few years and have managed to put away $50,000 in a GIC account with your bank. You are now in your middle years and want a better return than the 2% you are now receiving on your money, but you can't decide between stocks and real estate. You have read about the pros and cons of each, but still don't know what to do. Maybe the following will be of help.

Imagine you've purchased XYZ company, because BNN tells you that the share price should double in the next two years. To purchase $50,000 worth of shares you will have to spend all of your $50,000. There is no guarantee that your stock prices will go up and you understand that you might lose everything on this trade. You have absolutely no control over the management of the company and no insurance to protect your money if the company should go bankrupt.

But you got lucky, and the stock moved higher, closing the year with a 20% appreciation in value. That is a solid return of $10,000 on your investment after only one year. But the markets are skittish right now, and projections for the following year aren't as robust as you would like. This frustrates you; you can't project the value of your portfolio, or even be sure whether the company will still be around 5, 10, or 25 years from now.

On the other hand, what if you were to use that $50,000 to purchase real estate? If your credit is in good standing the banks would allow you to leverage their money in order to purchase $250,000 worth of real estate. You can't believe it. They are willing to give you four times the amount of money you saved for your purchase! How come your broker wasn't able to get you that kind of leverage for your stocks? You decide to buy two properties for $125,000 each with a $25,000 down payment.

The properties are in great locations, vacancy rates are low, and property values have modestly but consistently increased over the years. Your rents are more than enough to cover all your expenses and even leave you additional income (cash-flow) at the end of the month. In addition to that, your tenants' rents will have the mortgages completely paid off in 25 years.

Even in the worst-case scenario, if the values of the properties were to remain the same for 25 years, and rents did not increase; you would have turned your $50,000 into a cool $250,000. You also have the peace of mind knowing that if your property were to burn to the ground, your home insurance would cover the cost of building you a brand-new home. Isn't that amazing? So, let me see, where should I put my money?

Investment options

In addition to good and consistent leverage, there are a variety of investment strategies available in real estate to meet the needs of a variety of investor types. As I mentioned earlier, you would probably not go looking for cash-flow properties in the major urban markets unless you had deep pockets and a nose for value. A better strategy would be to buy for equity appreciation — which is what happens when an investor banks on the value of property increasing over time, so that when it is sold they will make a bigger profit. This strategy can significantly increase an investor's wealth if they get in and out at the right time. But it can also be devastating if your timing is off. You don't have to look any further than to our neighbours to the south to understand this important truth.

If you are particularly handy and have skills in the trades, the "fix and flip" might just be what you are looking for. This strategy is not for the faint of heart, as it will often require a lot of blood, sweat, and tears (your own) to transform what others have considered an eyesore into something of value that other people will want to buy. Another risk with this strategy is that it often requires more money to do the work needed than originally thought, so you will need to consider this carefully.

The strategy I love the most is the buy and hold for cash-flow. It is a great way to wealth, because if it is done correctly you will profit both when you buy and when you sell. The strategy is probably the most popular for investors looking for the path to financial freedom, defined as having cash-flow or passive income from your investments that exceed your monthly expenses. If monthly expenses equal $3,000 and your cash-flow from your real estate is equal to or greater than $3,000, then you are technically financially free. The bonus is that you also profit when you sell, both through the increased equity your tenants' rents have created and the appreciation of your real estate holdings.

Added Value

Unlike stocks, you can add value to real estate holdings. This is a significant benefit; it can turn an average property into an exceptional one. The great thing about added value is that it doesn't take significant dollars out of your pocket to dramatically improve the quality of your building and the rents you can command. For example, you might convert a portion of your unused front lawn to a parking lot and charge an extra premium on your rents for parking. You might provide your tenants the convenience of doing their laundry at home by purchasing a coin-operated washer and dryer. This will save them time and put more dollars in your pocket. You might even spend a few thousand to spruce up the place with a paint job and some affordable laminate flooring. Not a significant cost, yet one that might bring in an extra $50 to $100 in monthly rents.

Strong Yields

Real estate investors are always looking for strong and predictable returns; this allows them to sleep at night knowing that in time their efforts will bear fruit. If you are making your investment choices on sound fundamentals in rental markets that have seen steady job and population growth together with low vacancy rates, it is quite reasonable to expect returns of 7% to 20%. The great thing about real estate is that you don't have to guess what your returns will be, because you would have already analyzed the deal before your purchase.

Tax Advantages

Many tax advantages are available to those who invest in real estate. As I know absolutely nothing about tax law, I would suggest you speak with your accountant about the benefits available to wealth seekers who choose this vehicle. What I do know is that an investor can deduct various expenses associated with real estate ownership. You can also claim for depreciation, which is an annual amount allowed for wear and tear on your property to offset taxable income.

There is a wonderful saying by Don Campbell, president of the Real Estate Investment Network, about the power of real estate investing: that you should not wait to buy real estate, but instead buy real estate and wait. If you understand the significance of that statement, what I am about to share with you next will be easy to follow, even if the topic of real estate is new to you. All you need is basic multiplication skills.

Financial Fitness Formula

How many stocks would you need to own in order to become financially free, and could you determine with some degree of accuracy how much your portfolio would be worth in, say, 25 years? That is a very difficult question to answer even for a seasoned investor like the great Warren Buffett. I emphasized above that the extreme volatility in the stock market not only wreaks havoc with one's emotions, but can also wipe you out financially. It is this being up one day only to be down the next that makes it absolutely impossible to predict the health of your finances 25 years into the future.

But what if I asked you how many cash-flow investment properties you would need to own in order to be financially free, could you tell me? In addition, would you be able to tell me with some degree of accuracy the value of your real estate portfolio 25 years into the future? If you're not sure, the answer is a resounding yes, and this is probably the biggest reason 97% of all wealth is achieved through or held in real estate. The key to real estate riches is to understand a very simple formula: Financial freedom is achieved when cash-flow exceeds your monthly expenses.

A quick example will show you the formula in action. How much passive income (cash-flow) would you need for financial freedom if your monthly expenses were $3,000? The answer: you would need to earn $3,000 or more per month in passive income.

How many doors (units) or investment properties will you need to buy in order to get $3,000 per month in passive income? The answer would vary from one person to the next, as it is based on the amount of cash-flow you get from each investment. But if you have a minimum cash-flow target for each purchase you plan to make, it is easy to determine the exact number of properties you will need to purchase.

For our example we will assume that you will only buy properties that cash-flow a minimum of $150.00 per door. For some of you, this might not sound like a big deal, but with it you are $150.00 closer to getting out of the rat race and have your money working for you. If your target is $3,000 in passive monthly income and each door returns $150.00 a month, you will need to purchase 20 doors to reach your goal. I got this number by dividing $3,000 by $150.00. Those doors might come in any combination of single-family homes, duplexes, triplexes, etc. The type of building you decide to buy does not matter, what matters is you have a formula that will work every time.

I made the bold statement at the very beginning of the book that you could become financially free within five to ten years if you were willing to follow certain strategies. Let me show you how, using the example above.

If you need 20 doors to get to financial freedom, and your strategy is to buy duplexes in small-town Ontario, can you do the math to figure out how many duplexes you need to purchase? Of course you can: a duplex is a two-family dwelling that can be side by side, up and down, or front and back. Buying a duplex is the equivalent of buying two doors. Therefore, if you were to buy ten duplexes you would have achieved your goal of owning 20 doors.

If you bought only one duplex per year, you would reach your financial freedom goal in exactly ten years, providing your expenses have not gone up and you are still getting $150.00 per door. To achieve your goals in five years, all you would need to do is purchase an average of two duplexes per year.

So now you know if you follow the blueprint you will be able to retire in style and comfort, but how much will your portfolio be worth 25 years into the future? That is a good question, and this example will serve as additional support for why real estate is such a powerful vehicle to wealth.

Let's go back to the example we used earlier of buying 20 doors. You have managed to purchase your ten duplexes in five years — congratulations are in order and welcome to your financial freedom! The purchase price for each duplex was approximately $100,000, and you are carrying a total mortgage of $800,000. But you are not concerned, because the tenants' rents cover the cost of carry the mortgages and all expenses and provide you with a monthly cash-flow of $3,000. In 25 years you will be mortgage-free with $1,000,000 of equity in your properties.

Are you excited about your future? You should be. But hold on, it gets better. As the years passed, your property values were increasing by an average of 4% per year. In the hot Toronto and Vancouver markets, that might not be considered a great appreciation rate, but you are not investing in these markets and will gladly take 4%. This means that in 25 years of ownership, your properties have increased in value by 100%. You, my friend, have not $1,000,000 but $2,000,000 in real estate equity under your control: 4% X 25 years equals 100% appreciation.

Now you should really be excited. But wait — it gets even better than this. Come on, you think, you've to be kidding, how can it get any better?

Well, when you bought your property 25 years earlier you were getting $150.00 per door and that was good. But as each year passes, the government allows you to raise your rents a little to keep pace with inflation and the cost of living. Additionally, the steady decrease of your mortgage balance means less money is going to service debt and more money is going into your pocket as cash flow. You may have started out earning $3,000 in cash-flow, but that amount might be as much as $10,000 a month by the time your mortgages are paid off. Could you live comfortably on $10,000 a month knowing that this income doesn't come from you putting in hours, but from your money working on your behalf? I am sure I already know the answer.

To me having cash coming in every month like clockwork is what we should all be striving for. When money is no longer a concern, we can expand our lives to do more for others. One of the things I talk about throughout this book is the importance of leaving a legacy and making a difference. There are countless ways to impact people on our journey through life, and many of you have already achieved major milestones, leaving your mark indelibly in hearts and minds. But when it comes to leaving financial legacies, few in society make this a priority, and that needs to change.

As mentioned, I come from a family in which money was not discussed, simply because we didn't have it. There was no one to lend a hand when times were hard or offer advice on how to earn more so you wouldn't have to struggle through life. We had to learn things the hard way. Don't get me wrong, I am not complaining. In fact, I am proud of where I come from and the hardships I had to overcome, because it has toughened my fibre and made me the man I am today.

What I am trying to say is that we need to start putting greater emphasis and priority on gaining financial freedom, not for the things money can buy, but for all the things it can't. Money gives you options and allows you to live a comfortable life. Most importantly, it buys you back your time from the demands of the 9-to-5 job so that you can spend time with family and friends and live life to the fullest.

Chapter Thirteen

My Story

n 2002 I was living in a one-bedroom apartment located near Main and Danforth, close to the heart of the city. The apartment was decent, but I was certainly not in the best part of town. I was a few years into my teaching career and had expenses that kept me up nights wondering how I was ever going to get them under control. My net income after taxes was approximately $2,600, and I was burning $2,200 per month on expenses. I was extremely dejected, but I knew I had to continue working evenings and weekends at the nightclubs even though I had grown tired of the scene.

A friend of mine convinced me that the money I was paying for rent and utilities would be more than enough to cover a mortgage. I knew nothing about home ownership, and was worried that I would somehow mess things up closing the deal. But eventually I took a leap of faith and decided to purchase my first home.

I wasn't making a lot of money and was only able to qualify for a $200,000-dollar mortgage. Where was I going to find a house in Toronto for $200,000?

I was referred to a realtor by a family friend, and I laid out the specifics of what I was looking for. I wanted a bungalow or a "back-split" with separate entrances, two kitchens, two bathrooms, and living quarters [a **back-split is a house in which the floors are staggered, so that the "main" level of the house is halfway between the upper and lower floors**]. My mom was living in a rundown apartment building, and I hated visiting her there. The people were rude and had no respect for themselves or others, and I had promised her I would move her to a better place. I love my mom, but I was not about to buy a home and share the same living space with her. A single, good-looking young man like me needed to have his own private space (I'm sure you understand what I mean).

My agent and I looked far and wide, and every day our search kept pushing us further and further east. Finally we found a four-level back-split in Whitby, Ontario, with an above-ground pool and more than enough privacy and space to satisfy all my desires. Whitby hadn't been on my radar when I started looking, but after six weeks of searching I was tired. Our offer was accepted and in the summer of 2002 I became a homeowner.

I should have been happy, right? But I wasn't. I was still teaching in the city, leaving home by 7:15 a.m. to avoid traffic congestion on the 401. Getting home wasn't any better: I had to be on the highway before 4 p.m. to have any hope of missing the slow Conga line of cars heading east during the rush hour. Of course, I wasn't the only teacher living in the east; but for me, getting on the highway by 4 o'clock was next to impossible. I was coaching a number of teams at school, taking my principal's courses in the heart of the city, and attending karate classes three or four times a week.

I had purchased a home to relieve some of the financial pressure I was facing, but I wasn't any further ahead. My commute to and from the city seven days a week was proving quite costly, because my gas-guzzling, six-cylinder Pontiac Grand Prix was burning holes in my pocket.

I had no quality of life to speak of. I was leaving home at 7:15 a.m. and getting back at 10:30 p.m. This gave me just enough time for a quick bite before bed in order to start all over again. I was losing touch with many of my friends, who balked at the long drive to my house. Some would jokingly say that in order to come see me they would need to pack a lunch. These statements although said jokingly, forced me to reflect on what I was doing. Six months later I made a call to my agent to put my house up for sale.

During the time I lived in Whitby, I had taken out a loan against my line of credit and renovated the basement into a separate living space. That improvement increased the value of my home and attracted a buyer two days after my house was listed. A buyer I might add, who was more than happy to pay me my asking price. I made a small profit on the sale, paid off my loan, and bought a 2002 Honda Civic with cash. Did I tell you I hate owing money?

I bought my second home in Scarborough only a few minutes from my work at a reasonable price. It had the features I was looking for, but would require some work to get my space renovated and up to my standards. I asked my agent if he had any advice for me as a new homeowner. "Pay off your mortgage as quickly as you can," was his response. I didn't know how I was going to do that, but I kept it in mind as something worth exploring.

My mortgage was with a bank known for their flexible prepayment privileges and step program. A *step mortgage* gives you access to a secured line of credit against your home. The benefit is that any amount of equity you pay down below 80% loan to value is made available as a line of credit. This is great: as you reduce your mortgage balance you have a low-interest loan available that you can draw from should you need it. This would prove to be priceless when the time came to show the banks where my down payments for investment properties were coming from.

In 2006, my sister Audrey and I started discussing real estate as our vehicle for wealth. She had recently bought her first home, and we decided we would purchase a condo together. We drove all over the city looking at the different projects going up, but the price for many of them seemed beyond our reach. I finally came across a new development that fit our budget, and after looking at the floor plans we pulled the trigger and got into the deal. Now all we needed to do was find the $50,000 for the down payment and closing costs. No problem. I had been aggressively paying down my mortgage and had access to $60,000 in a secured line of credit. We would be okay.

It would be another two years before the condo was ready, and it was at this point in my life that I started going to seminars to learn all I could about investing in real estate. I would spend weekend after weekend attending the various seminars held across the city to increase my knowledge and to network with others. When you are going after something, you've got to keep it in front of you, not in the rear-view mirror.

During one of these weekend seminars I met a gentleman who told me there was a program that could help me pay off my mortgage in as little as half to one-third the time. I couldn't believe my ears. That was exactly what I wanted to do. I had never forgotten the advice of my realtor to pay off my mortgage as soon as possible. We exchanged numbers, and he called soon after to invite me to watch a webinar on this particular strategy. I watched the program, but I wasn't buying it — not because it wasn't good, but because the price tag was a little too rich for my blood.

Nevertheless, the general idea was priceless. It was a way to leverage the bank's money by borrowing from my low-interest line of credit to pay off my high-interest mortgage. I understood the concept well enough that I started experimenting with it on my own.

There is a saying that what you focus on the longest becomes the strongest, and the next event to unfold has made me a strong believer in this "law of attraction." One afternoon while checking my email, I came across an invitation to a real estate seminar. Now, I am very careful to keep my personal emails away from my work account, but somehow this particular one found its way into my work email folder. It was from the Thornhill Wealth Forum, and I read it in total disbelief:

Join us this Saturday at the Bayview Country Club for two dynamic speakers
You will learn how to create financial freedom through real estate and how to pay off your mortgage in 1/2 to 1/3 the time
Please RSVP to Thornhill Wealth Forum
Azhar Laher

How the heck did this get into my inbox, what is Thornhill Wealth, and who is this Azhar Laher? By the time I had read the email a second time I knew I couldn't afford to pass up this opportunity. I thought this message was meant specifically for me. This couldn't be a coincidence.

I attended the meeting the following Saturday and introduced myself to Azhar. He could not explain how his invitation had gotten into my inbox but was glad to see me.

I found a seat and took out my journal as the first speaker began. He described an incredible program that allowed individuals to take charge of their lives by dramatically reducing the time needed to pay off mortgages and other consumer debts in half or one-third the regular time. He was delivering the same presentation I had seen on the webinar a few weeks ago! This time I was taking notes like crazy, because I understood the power behind this concept and knew I had to try it.

There was a brief networking opportunity after the first speaker to allow those in attendance to mingle and exchange cards.

The second speaker arrived and we all took our seats. Her topic was creating financial freedom through real estate. I opened my journal to a new page and wrote down her name, Mrs. Paola Breda. There was nothing flashy about her, she was down-to-earth and spoke of the obstacles she'd overcome to get to where she was and why it was important for all of us to create financial freedom. I liked her from the get-go, but it was her story of personal triumph and her desire to give back to others that sealed the deal.

She had bought a property in Muskoka, despite everyone, including the bankers and their grandmothers, telling her it wasn't possible. She explained that when you have a white-hot desire for a thing, there are no insurmountable obstacles. As her presentation went on, I realized I was in the right room, at the right time, with the right person. When she revealed that she was teaching a weekend course on real estate investing in Muskoka, I signed up immediately. I knew nothing about her background or whether she was credible, but something in my gut told me I needed to learn from this lady. I paid my $1,000 and went to Muskoka with total faith that everything would be all right.

I came away from her real estate course more confused than ever — everything she taught was way over my head — but true to her word, she did not abandon us after the course and offered monthly meetings and email correspondence that pushed us to get off our seats and make offers. I was venturing into the unknown, but there was no turning back because I thought this path was definitely for me.

Getting my first deal wasn't easy. There were many lonely nights on the road when I felt like giving up. But a little voice kept me awake, moving toward my goals, and I remember my very first accepted offer on a duplex in Windsor and how excited I was to be purchasing my first cash-flow property.

I had my agent set up the inspection and drove four hours to Windsor to have a look and talk to the inspector. We hadn't even gone through half of the house before I threw in the towel, paid him, and was on my lonely four-hour drive back home. I called my sister and told her the bad news that the deal was not going to happen because the inspection was brutal. The building was in poor shape, requiring at least $15,000 in repairs. I was disappointed but not discouraged.

Paola continued her push for us to make offers and find a deal. I was working my butt off checking MLS (multiple listing services) listings every night and starting to feel the pressure. Finally I got a lead on a few properties in London, Ontario, and was relieved that this drive would take only two hours each way. Another bonus was that I would not be travelling alone. I had formed a really good friendship with a few investors at the club, and Sadhana and I were both interested in London.

We had three showings booked that afternoon, and by the time we left the third house we were absolutely disgusted by the condition of the units. Sadhana and I sat in a little restaurant after we had thoroughly sanitized ourselves to discuss our findings. How could anyone live in such conditions? More importantly, how could they show their house in that condition to potential investors? As I sat there, I started to question if this was really what I wanted to do. I could never allow my property to fall apart like those we had just seen, or allow tenants to do as they pleased in my unit. I wanted to buy real estate in order to provide affordable housing for people and to create financial freedom for myself. I didn't want to be a slumlord.

Sadhana and I drove home much more subdued than we had been on the trip to London. Getting home, I thanked her for keeping me company and went back to the drawing board. This was not going to be easy, I kept on telling myself. Every time I would say that, I heard the voice of Les Brown telling me easy was not an option and successful people were willing to fail their way to success — but to be honest, I was beginning to lose a bit of pep in my step.

Despite several unsuccessful offers and travelling hundreds of miles only to come up empty-handed, I was still analyzing deals and hoping for a break. About three weeks after my London trip, I connected with a realtor in Cornwall. I didn't know where Cornwall was, but I knew it was a four-hour drive east, toward Ottawa. I remember asking why all these cash-flow properties were all located in God's land.

My realtor would send me listings of all the duplexes and triplexes on the market, and I would spend hours doing spreadsheets on every one of them. I knew none of the shortcuts investors used to assess whether a building cash-flowed and would require a more in-depth analysis. I definitely had a great deal to learn about this business for sure. Fortunately you won't have to make my mistakes. Here is the short formula for analyzing if a deal is worth further investigation. If the gross monthly rental income is greater than 10% of the purchase price you could have a winning property on your hands that meet your cash-flow requirements. If the rents are lower than 10% of the purchase price you might want to consider looking elsewhere.

Eventually, after about eight hours poring over spreadsheets, I found four promising properties, and asked my realtor to set up appointments for me to see them. It was raining that Friday afternoon when I left Toronto for Cornwall. The only company I had for this eight-hour turnaround drive was the voices of Earl Nightingale (*Lead the Field*) and Napoleon Hill (*Think and Grow Rich*) on my CD player. I call this trip a turnaround because I would be turning right around after seeing the properties to head back to Toronto.

I pulled into Cornwall around 4:30 that afternoon, and by 6:30 had seen all the properties. Two continued to show promise, so we drew up offers and submitted them to the seller's agent. I thanked my realtor, and drove to a restaurant to have dinner by myself before heading home — a first for me — and as I sat there alone with my thoughts I kept asking myself if this was really worth it. Did I really have what it took to see this through, or should I call it quits and settle for what I already had as my friend had suggested?

Soon I was back on the road listening to Napoleon Hill telling me, "What the mind of man can conceive and believe, he can achieve." 'Mr. Hill, I hope you are right, I certainly hope you are right,' I thought. The drive was long and tiring, and I found myself drifting off from time to time. To overcome that urge, I would roll the window down and crank up the voice of Napoleon Hill. I finally arrived home about 1:00 a.m. exhausted and craving my pillow.

The next day the phone rang. It was my realtor calling with the good news that both my offers had been accepted!

I pumped my fist in the air. "Yes!" I felt good about the offers I had submitted on the two buildings, and knew that my hard work was about to pay off. All the negative thoughts that had been following me for the past three months were gone.

My elation was short-lived. We ordered the inspections, and within a few days I got a copy of the reports. I spent a good hour going over the entire thing on the phone with the inspector. The electrical was outdated and needed repairs, the plumbing was not up to code, there was some asbestos found in the basement that would need removal, the roof required immediate repairs ... and on and on and on.

I thanked the inspector and asked him where to send the cheque. Then I called the realtor and told her to scrap the deal because the inspection reports were not good.

What would you do at this point? Would you throw in the towel? Wouldn't you be tempted to accept things as they were and feel justified that at least you had tried and failed? I had spent countless hours on the highway by myself looking for that elusive deal that might turn my financial life around and could not find it. I asked myself how many more miles and hours alone I was willing to commit to going after my dreams?

These thoughts raced through my mind day and night, but every time I thought of throwing in the towel I would remember my why: to give my family more than enough so they could enjoy the finer things in life and not just hear of others' stories, to be in a position to give to others in abundance beyond my physical reach, and to leave an inheritance for my children's children.

I had taken Paola's course in November 2008. Here it was the end of April 2009, and despite all my efforts and the constant encouragement I had yet to find a deal. When would this drought end? To get my mind onto something more positive, I bought a ticket for a conference by motivational speaker Tony Robbins in Toronto. The place was jammed with enthusiastic participants eager to be in the presence of this man, who appeared to be larger than life. I was blown away by his passion on the subject of personal development and going after your dreams. I felt right at home, because I was living the message he was delivering.

At intermission I checked my phone to see if there was anything pressing I needed to respond to. One email jumped out at me; it simply said, "Call me pronto." It was from a realtor from Sault Ste. Marie I had met several months earlier. Bill and I had developed a good relationship, and I would check in with him regularly to see if there was any activity in his city. His usual response was, "Not much happening right now, Courtney. There have been a few listings, but they're all garbage and not worth your time." This time was different.

"Hey, Bill, this is Courtney how are things going?"

"Everything is fine, Courtney. Did you get my email?"

"Yes that is why I am calling. You said to call pronto, so here I am."

"Good. I sent out a mass email and wasn't sure who would respond, and since you got to me first you are the lucky one."

"Why is that?" I asked.

"Well, a new listing came on the market today, and I don't think it will last. I believe they listed it under price, so we should move on it right away. I will get in there in the morning and fire off a few pictures for you to look at."

I had never done a deal with Bill, but our relationship over the phone and via email had grown strong and I trusted him more than anyone else I had dealt with so far.

Everything felt right about this deal. Here I was at a conference listening to one of the giants on living purposefully, and now in the intermission I was speaking to a realtor more than 700 kilometres away about buying my first investment property. I couldn't have scripted it any better.

To make a long story short, the deal went through, and I was now officially a real estate investor! Three weeks later I found myself with yet another opportunity to purchase a property, and as you might imagine I was beside myself when that deal closed too.

It had taken me almost six months of hard work to find my first deal, and only three short weeks to find the second. This was absolutely incredible. The obstacles that had stood in my way had been removed, and I was learning new things about the world of investing with every purchase.

My life has changed significantly since that first purchase. I have made new friends in real estate, formed partnerships with incredible people to complete deals, and am on course to live the life I have always imagined possible for me. I am living in a new house in a community of my choosing, and, still using the early strategies, I have learned to eliminate my biggest debt in half to one-third the time while purchasing additional properties. My 30-year mortgage has since been reduced to eight years, resulting in a total savings of almost $200,000 in interest payments. Most importantly, I am transferring what I have learned to others, because I believe that teaching is one of the best ways to serve others.

I have often wondered where I would be today if I had given up on my dreams after coming up empty in Cornwall. Someone once said that life's obstacles are the admission price one has to pay for success. I certainly met with obstacles, but fortunately I had a new-found philosophy that would not allow me to tap out simply because the going was tough.

What obstacles stand between you and the goals you have set for yourself? Are you willing to pay the price by attacking each one with courage and determination? You must develop the perspective that obstacles are not meant to stop you, they are put in your way to test your resolve.

This chapter has hopefully illustrated the importance, not only of thinking outside the box and finding multiple streams of income to secure your wealth, but also of developing the right philosophy for success in all aspects of your life. Success is not a destination but a process, the progressive realization of a worthy goal. You are successful as long as you keep moving toward your dreams. This means, too, that you should not rest too long once you have achieved any particular aim, but set your sights on new ones that will challenge you to *live full and die empty* (Les Brown).

Remember that real estate wealth requires a long-term commitment, so you must be leery of those who promise you the world in as little as 30 days. We live in a microwave society in which people want results immediately. They often forget that there is a cultivation period between planting the seeds and reaping the harvest. People who meet with failure often overlook this most important period and forget to nurture the seeds they plant. They are looking for the quick fix or the overnight success. You cannot rush success. You attract success by the person you become.

If we have learned anything from our history books, it is that those who fail in life are quick to give up after the first signs of failure or defeat. They are not willing to adjust their sails, tweak their plans, and keep trying. Successful people, on the other hand, understand that the probability of success increases exponentially every time you meet with failure and are able to bounce back. They surround themselves with those who share their vision and are willing to fail their way to success.

You have all the tools needed to take your life to the next level. The question is whether you have the courage to "step into your greatness," as Les Brown would say, and join the 5% at the top of the ladder.

Chapter Fourteen

Charity: Give and you shall receive

Each of us will one day be judged by our standard of life, not by our standard of living; by our measure of giving, not by our measure of wealth; by our simple goodness, not by seeming greatness.

—William Arthur Ward

We've often heard that the measure of a man is not based on the millions he accumulates throughout his life, but by the goodness of his character and the difference he makes in the lives of others. The late great Jim Rohn, one of the greatest speakers on personal development and business success, died an extremely wealthy man. Rohn was a man of impeccable character who lived his life for others. When he died few remembered or even cared about the mega-millions he had accumulated over his 40-year career in sales and business.

What people remembered were the stories he masterfully crafted that inspired millions to change their philosophy. His legacy will live on and impact generations to come, long after his millions have been exhausted. This should be the goal of all mature adults, to create our own lives by design, so that even after we have departed our story will live on in others.

As a young man growing up in "the projects," I had no exposure to the Jim Rohns, the Zig Ziglars, or the Les Browns of the world. My circle of influence was extremely limited, consisting of individuals who rarely if ever picked up a book or listened to educational audios. I had no thought of being a difference-maker to others and giving to charity was not one of my priorities. If anything, I was the one hoping to be the beneficiary of someone else's charity. Don't get me wrong, I had plenty of compassion and kindness for those less fortunate. I just couldn't help them financially.

Fortunately for me, my early upbringing in the church instilled in me the importance of giving back to others. One of the early lessons I received was that God loves a cheerful giver, and has blessed man with two hands, one to receive and one to give. I later learned that giving did not have to be monetary. Once I understood this, I made sure I adopted the philosophy and did all that I could to help others.

The act of giving is incredibly powerful, not only for the one receiving, but also for the one giving. It has the power to start the process that can unlock the doors to untold treasures.

The Bible says those who give shall receive, but you have to give with a willing heart, not for the purpose of getting that future reward. That is not how the law works. You must give with gladness in your heart.

It was Zig Ziglar who said, *"You can have everything in life that you want if you will just help enough other people get what they want."* He was right; when you start operating from a place of total kindness and love for others you will be amazed at what the universe brings into your life.

The Power of Giving

> *We make a living by what we get. We make a life by what we give.*
> —Winston Churchill

In my early years the concept of giving was not engrained in my DNA. In fact, I used to think I didn't have enough — so why should I give to others? Later I came to realize that I was just making excuses and operating from a poverty mindset. I had been conditioned early to believe my family didn't have enough when it came to money. So as I started to earn my own, I held it tight for fear of losing it. It wasn't that I lacked the resources to be of assistance, I just didn't want to part with my money.

My story is not unique. I believe most people still see the world through a poverty lens. Their failure to accept the natural law of the universe, that as you sow so shall you reap, has kept them in perpetual servitude, often in dead-end jobs they despise. But chances are you who are reading this book, are not one of them. You realize that it is far better to be in a position to give than on the receiving end of others' charity. This is yet one more reason for you to get your finances in order. When money is no longer an issue, you can give graciously and bless those less fortunate than yourself.

Here's some advice that might change your life for the better. You don't have to listen. But at least in my own experience, the value you receive will be far greater than that which you give. Here it is:

Find a way to serve as many as possible and your rewards will be multiplied tenfold.

I can honestly say that everything I have accomplished so far in my life has been because of the assistance of others. To be sure, I had a burning desire to do more with my life and move in the direction of my goals, but the mentorship and the coaching provided along the way was priceless.

As my life and career started to flourish, it seemed that every obstacle or challenge was easily surmounted as one person after another came to my aid at exactly the time I needed guidance and support. It was a very perplexing thing, but the more I started to read and attend seminars the more I started to understand the universal law that our outside world is merely a reflection of who we are on the inside. To put it another way, what we think in our minds and do with our hearts for others will also be done unto us. You've likely heard this before as "What goes around comes around."

You see, once I got rid of the idea that I couldn't afford to help others and developed a new philosophy of giving, my life started to change. I was now making a difference in the lives of others by giving of my time, money, and talents. These acts in and of themselves were not a big deal for me, but they were a big deal to those on the receiving end. More than that, my new outlook brought me tremendous joy and satisfaction, knowing I was bringing sunshine into others' lives.

I had been sowing good seeds, and the serendipitous assistance of my mentors and coaches was merely the universe rewarding me for having enriched the lives of others. I can't explain how this thing works. That isn't my concern. All I can tell you is that it does. Some things I have learned not to question any more, I simply do them.

Charity is in you to give, but a word of caution here. You can't predict just how what goes around will come back around to you. Don't make the mistake of doing a good deed and then sitting back waiting for rewards. You can't give $100.00 to charity and expect a $1,000-dollar cheque in the mail the following week. Give and expect nothing in return. If it comes from the heart, you will be rewarded, but it might not be dollars for dollars.

Let me share a story with you before moving on. After graduating university and hanging up my football cleats, I took up softball. I enjoyed the game, but the quick, explosive runs required to chase down fly balls as a centre fielder played havoc with my hamstrings. Eventually I had to turn my back on the sport and hang up those cleats as well.

After a week pondering my next athletic challenge, I decided to try my hand at the martial arts, which had interested me. What I didn't know was the impact my decision would have on my life. I grew to absolutely love the sport, and although I have suffered setbacks over the years, the rewards have been invaluable. As I moved up the ranks and earned my black belt (in our dojo you earn your belts, nothing is given to you), I was asked if I would be interested in teaching a new-parents class that we would be offering. I said yes after thinking it over — for about five seconds. I know, you're thinking: *This guy takes forever to make decisions, how the heck does he make it through the day?*

One of the reasons I agreed was that I knew it was time for me to give back to the club. Secondly, I knew that by teaching others my own skills would be sharpened as I would be forced to break things down into manageable, bite-sized pieces for those just starting martial arts.

The gym had become my second home, and my family (my sister and my mother) began to question why I was giving so much of my time without being compensated. They both felt I should be getting paid for my time, effort, and talent. I explained that the club was growing, and this was my way of saying thanks for all who had helped me develop. Most importantly, I said, it felt good especially seeing other's progress, knowing you had a hand in moving them along. I told them not to worry, that my work wouldn't go unrewarded, because kindness, like a boomerang, always returns.

Two weeks later I heard my mom complaining about her toes. As a diabetic she suffered from pain and swelling in her feet and had great difficulty finding relief. "Your daughter is a nurse," I told her, "Why don't you see if she can help you connect with a doctor at the hospital?" "She doesn't have time and she is always busy." I listened with a heavy heart, because I had heard her complaining for several months.

But then a light bulb went on, and I made a phone call to Carlos, one of my karate students, who just happened to be one of three doctors who attended my classes.

Carlos wrote up a requisition for my mother, and less than two weeks later we were sitting in the office of one of the best foot specialists in Pickering. How come? Is it simply a coincidence or is there something greater at work? You tell me. For months she had been complaining and going from one doctor to the next, never being satisfied with their answers; and because of me sowing good seeds we were now sitting with a specialist.

The specialist confirmed that my mom had arthritis and diabetes, and that a diabetic shoe would provide some relief. But here is where the story gets interesting. My mother had suffered a childhood injury to her right shin that had never healed properly. She had been treated by many doctors over the years, but her concerns had always been dismissed. This specialist didn't take the injury lightly however, and referred us to Sunnybrook for a biopsy. Several visits and two biopsies later, we were told that my mother had skin cancer and would require an operation.

She had the surgery, made a full recovery, and is healthy to this day.

I am extremely grateful to Carlos for giving my mom that initial referral. Without his intervention it is uncertain how things would have played out for us.

I don't believe in luck. I believe each act of kindness and service you render for others will return tenfold to you. Our time on this planet is not infinite. In fact, it is extremely short. When your time finally comes to pass from this life to the next, be sure that the measure of your success is based on the lives you have touched.

How much should you give?

The good book (the Bible) tells us we should give the first 10% of our monthly income to God. But what if you can't afford to give that much? Should you wait until you can and give nothing in the meantime? Of course not! What you need to do is begin where you are until you can get where you want to be.

Giving to charity is no different than saving for your retirement. You don't get to a 20% rate of saving overnight. It takes time to develop the discipline and the outlook needed to make this your reality. You need to approach your tithing and charity in the same manner, by starting where you are comfortable. If parting with 5% of your monthly income to support a charity is a challenge, then start with 2% or 3% and take it from there.

For many of you this will prove much easier said than done, and I certainly understand that. But I am sure that if you follow the principles I have outlined, you will be able to donate 10% or more to your charity of choice within five to ten years. Imagine the tremendous impact you could have on the lives of others when money is no longer a concern. This is why it is so critically important to create a financially fit future so you can be in a position to bless others.

If you have not already adopted the giving philosophy, don't worry, the best of your life is yet to come. Don't be concerned about the size of your contributions to others when you are getting started. It is not the amount that matters, but the building of the philosophy and the development of the simple habits that will lead to success and a blessed life.

I would suggest that, like saving for your retirement, you get started immediately. Waiting until the big money comes in before giving to others is a recipe for disaster. It is much easier to develop the habit of giving a dime out of a dollar than it is to give $10,000 out of $100,000. It is the same amount, so what's the difference? Well, if you have not developed the habit of giving 10 cents out of your dollar it is very unlikely you will give up the $10,000 out of your $100,000.

Many people make the mistake of thinking that if all they have to give is $2, they should feel embarrassment. But what if your $2 represents a greater percentage of your earnings than the donation of a man who gave $20,000 — are you not making a greater sacrifice in terms of your level of income?

An interesting Bible story illustrates this concept beautifully. Jesus and his disciples were sitting at the church treasury observing the multitude putting money into the treasury. Many rich people were putting in large sums. But he observed a poor widow who came forward and put in two small copper coins, the equivalent of one penny. Jesus called his disciples and said to them, "Truly I say to you, this poor widow put in more than all the contributors to the treasury; for they all put in out of their surplus, but she, out of her poverty, put in all she owned, all she had to live on."

What a powerful story about the importance of giving! Her selfless act was recognized by Jesus at the church treasury, and one can only imagine the blessings that would have been showered upon her. It isn't the amount that is important, but the act of giving with a willing heart that will unlock the doors of possibilities for all.

Make Giving Automatic

It is far easier to have monthly deductions withdrawn from your bank account or your credit card than to try and manage it on your own. For one thing, most people lack the discipline needed to write cheques on a monthly basis to their charities, because it is time-consuming and a bit inconvenient. For another, the regular grind of our daily lives has a way of overwhelming the most organized individual from time to time. This can often lead those with the best of intentions to forget to make donations. Repeat this mistake a few months in a row, and before you know it you have developed the habit of not giving regularly.

There is one more reason why you want to make your giving automatic. If you are writing cheques on a monthly basis or giving when you think you can afford to do so, what will you do when the going gets tough? Life is like the seasons, and you will have many winters in which your resources will be depleted and you just don't think you can survive. Will you continue to pull out your chequebook, or will you be tempted to hold off on your contributions until brighter days appear?

For most people the answer is simple: "I am going to stop my contributions until things get better." Here is the problem with that philosophy: if things don't get better in a few months or in a year, you would have lost the habit of giving to others. You cannot predict how long your winters will last; but with 100% certainty you know that your winters will be followed by spring and with it the hope of better days ahead if you sow the right seeds. You must protect the good habits from the weeds constantly trying to choke them out.

There have been times when I ran into unexpected expenses that stretched me beyond my comfort zone for months, and I thought I needed to cancel my charitable donations. But I finally decided "This too shall pass." Winter couldn't last forever; my spring was just around the corner. All I needed to do was hang on a little longer and work on my plans so when the next winter came I would be better prepared.

So I stuck with my plan, and though times were hard I resisted the temptation to cancel my contributions. I would not allow the weeds of self-doubt to creep back into my mind and mess with my new-found philosophy. Neither should you.

Ways of Giving

There are many ways of donating help to those in need. Unfortunately most people associate charity with dollars only. When you look at the amount of unsolicited mail, TV commercials, and infomercials asking for monetary donations, it is easy to see why the majority in society make this connection. But, as mentioned earlier, money is not the only medium of value transfer. It is the quickest and most convenient, but sometimes what is needed is something far more precious.

Giving money is easy. You pull out a $20.00 bill or maybe write a $200.00 cheque, send it to your local charity, and you are done. "That was easy — it's out of the way now," and you feel good because you know your funds will be making a difference.

But what if you don't have money to spare? What if *you* are one of those in need? Is there nothing you can do to be of service?

Well, you command something far more precious than money — your time. In fact, this is the most valuable commodity you possess, because once you use it up, it is gone forever. There are organizations in your community that have all the money they need to fund their programs, but unfortunately they don't have enough volunteers to do the physical work needed to meet the demands of those they serve.

So give of your time if money is an issue for you at present. Your time does have a monetary value. It's entirely possible you will be giving greater value than the man or woman who donates $100.00. Think of it. What monetary value do you place on your time? Perhaps an hour is worth $30.00, $50.00, or even $100.00.

So if your time is worth $30.00 an hour and you are willing to donate five hours a week to a local charity, it would be the equivalent of you donating $30.00 X 5 or $180.00 every week to a worthy cause. Can you do that? Can you find a way to serve others for a few hours a week? I am sure you can, you just have to decide on the charity and dive in.

As you can tell from this chapter, I strongly believe in the power of giving back. Therefore, what frustrates me more than anything else is the apathy of those who sit back and collect fat cheques from our government and do nothing of value to earn it — healthy adults who would rather spend their time hanging out on the street corners day after day doing absolutely nothing with their lives. While you and I go to work every day and pay taxes enabling these loafers to receive handouts from our government.

It is said that God helps those who help themselves, and I only wish our government would have the courage to make this part of their mandate for giving social assistance to healthy, capable Canadians who are bleeding the system not because they can't work, but because they choose not to.

Here is what I would love to see implemented. If you were in need and couldn't find gainful employment, you would have to donate your time to local organizations and take courses to improve your skills and employability. Not only would this increase the self-esteem and self-worth of those receiving assistance, but it would provide the human resources needed by the thousands of charities that are desperately low on volunteers. In addition, you and I would feel better about the state of our country and economy, because we would know that our dollars were being used to educate and bring more people with employable skills into the market. Maybe someone in government will read this book and bring it up in the House. One can only hope.

William Penn said: "I expect to pass through life but once. If therefore, there be any kindness I can show, or any good thing I can do to any fellow being, let me do it now, and not defer or neglect it, as I shall not pass this way again." Are you doing enough? Are you serving others with the incredible life you have been given?

Chapter Fifteen

The Blueprint

Congratulations! You have made it to the end of this book, and I want to thank you for spending part of your valuable time reading it. As you can see, I have not shared any new ideas on how to secure wealth for your brighter tomorrow. There are no new ideas, only different ways of expressing the same ones. The ideas are basic, but together they form the blueprint for your financial success.

The most fundamental of them is the understanding that you must have the mindset for attracting wealth. *Remember, where your attention goes your energy flows.* Far too many people spend their days focusing on what they don't have, instead of focusing on what they want in their lives. If you are in this group, you must make changes. You cannot continue to operate from a deficit mentality when it comes to the money game. You need to see yourself as worthy and having the ability to attract abundance. This shift in how you see your world is essential if you are ever going to achieve financial fitness.

With the right mindset you will no longer spend everything you earn, but adopt the outlook that a part of all you earn is yours to keep. This is essential, because in order for you to be trusted with more, you have to demonstrate to others that you can handle the small amounts before the big money comes in.

You will need to guard your money like a lion. You can't afford to lose your principal chasing *"champagne wishes and caviar dreams."* This is a recipe for disaster, and will most likely leave you filled with regret and embarrassment at the end of the day. There are thousands of get-rich-quick opportunities designed to take money out of your pocket and line the pockets of those who promote them. Stay disciplined and seek expert counsel from those who understand how to safeguard their money while putting it in investments that generate a handsome return.

Remember that profits are better than wages, and those who really flourish in the money game are constantly looking for opportunities to create multiple streams of income. Your goal is to generate additional income streams, not by trading your time for money but by driving one of the three vehicles to wealth so your cash-flow rolls in and your time-freedom rolls out. Time is our most precious resource, and we cannot continue to spend it without thought, even if we are able to take home a few extra dollars at the end of the week. Money should be working for you and not the other way around. It is said that money makes a poor master, but an excellent servant; so put it to work 24/7 so it can multiply and bear additional fruit.

As you start exploring ways of creating more wealth in your life, you will come across many people who tell you money is not important. All I can say is that kind of thinking is designed to keep you in perpetual servitude. In my early years, I held the same beliefs about money, but today I am a different man and know the importance of money in helping overcome the hardships of life.

To be sure, money is not the most important thing in life, and we have already established that in this book; but it is important and should be respected because of the choices it provides. It allows you to live a comfortable life, and where possible be in a position to bless others beyond the reach of your physical presence. When you are able to free yourself from the shackles of your 9-to-5 job, you can live as you see fit and impact others in many wonderful ways. The principles of multiple streams of income, along with the others mentioned in the previous chapters, have been used to unlock the doors of countless riches for generations past and are still being used today.

You might be asking yourself, if these ideas have been taught for hundreds of years, why do millions continue to struggle for survival? The answer is simple. They are comfortable where they are and not willing to take the actions needed to get better results.

The teaching of a lesson does not guarantee that learning has occurred. Learning requires practical application of the theory, and this can only occur if the student decides to take decisive action to test the soundness of what has been taught. Learning is a process that requires doing and refining, then doing again until one achieves success. You can't just read the books. All the theory in the world won't help unless it is coupled with action.

We educators understand that the most significant person in the classroom is the teacher. He or she is charged not only with the responsibility of teaching lessons that will engage students, but more importantly with ensuring that learning is taking place. However, outside the classroom, in the realm of personal finance, no one will be chasing after you to make sure you exercise the habits needed to win the game. No teacher will call your parents and tell them you failed to put a solid financial plan together for your future success. In the real world (life's classroom) there is no makeup test, and cramming the night before will not get you the results you want. In the real world your results come last and your final mark will be either a pass or a fail.

The key that can unlock the most stubborn of doors already resides in you. It is the desire to be more, so you can do more and have abundance in your life. That desire will open any door that stands between you and your dreams.

We have all made errors in our judgment when it comes to our finances. Some of us learned from those errors, read the books, attended the seminars, and put better plans together. Others have failed to change course. They continue to spend more than they earn, and do not have a savings plan or even think beyond the immediate moment. They continue to live a lie — to family, friends, and co-workers — pretending everything is okay. They dismiss the warning bells getting louder and louder with the urgent message that they might be doomed to a life of mediocrity.

I must confess I had reservations about sharing my failures with the world, but then I thought it could do a lot of good. My early failures might serve as a warning to others. You will not have to repeat my mistakes to understand the pain and regret one feels after losing tens of thousands because of greed and ignorance. Luckily my mistakes didn't cripple me, and for that I am grateful.

It's inevitable that we all must encounter the storms of life and maybe you are experiencing them right now. Take comfort knowing no storm last forever. However, in order to withstand them, you must have a greater pull in front of you. Let that pull be a brighter financial future. You owe it to yourself to live your life on the highest rung of the financial ladder.

To Your Success

With gratitude,

Courtney Carroll

Bibliography

Bach, David. *The Automatic Millionaire*. Toronto, Ontario: Doubleday Canada, 2003.

Clason, George. *The Richest Man in Babylon*. Signet, 1977.

Campbell, Don, Peter Kinch, Barry McGuire, and Russell Westcott. *97 Tips for Canadian Real Estate Investors*. Mississauga, Ontario: Wiley, 2006.

Green, Alexander. *The Gone Fishin' Portfolio*. Hobeken, New Jersey: Wiley, 2008.

Hill, Napoleon. *Think & Grow Rich*. Mineola, New York: Dover Publications, Inc, 2007.

J.Stanley, Thomas, and William D. Dankos. *The Millionaire Next Door*. New York, NY: Pocket Books, 1998.

Kiyosaki, Robert, and Sharon Lechter. *Rich Dad Poor Dad*. Business Plus, 2000.

Olson, Jeff. *The Slight Edge*. Lake Dallas, Texas: Success Books, 2005.

Rohn, Jim, and Chris Widener. *Twelve Pillars*. Dallas, Texas: Jim Rohn and Chris Widener International, 2005, 2010.

Trudeau, Kevin. *Debt Cures*. Phoenix, AZ: Equity Press, 2008.

Ziglar, Zig. *Over The Top*. Nashville, Tennessee: Thomas Nelson, 1994.

Index